SUCCESSFUL MARKETING RESEARCH

*The Complete Guide
to Getting and Using
Essential Information
About Your Customers
and Competitors*

EDWARD L. HESTER

JOHN WILEY & SONS, INC.
New York • Chichester • Brisbane • Toronto • Singapore

ISBN 0-471-12381-1
ISBN 0-471-12380-3 (paper)

Printed in the United States of America

10 9 8 7 6 5 4 3 2 1

CONTENTS

CONTENTS

CONTENTS

CONTENTS

ACKNOWLEDGMENTS

For many, the business of writing is a lonely one. For me, it certainly is. Writing requires a withdrawal from distractions so as to concentrate on selecting material, fitting the sections and paragraphs together, and making words flow smoothly.

To me, it feels like being at the bottom of a well. From that position, your view of the everyday world becomes very limited, and you quickly stop noticing what is going on around you. Conversation drops off. Taking a long walk gets you nowhere except back to the same paragraph you left. From all the hours sitting in front of a computer, your bottom widens; your belly drops; you develop a chronic neck ache; and you gain weight because you snack all the time.

While I was writing this book, meals were lowered to me daily by my wife, Pat. Thanks, dear, for the patience and encouragement. Advice and progress checks were periodically called to me by my friend and editor at John Wiley & Sons, Mike Hamilton. Thanks for the helpful advice, support, and education on the publishing business. I couldn't have done this without you.

For his assistance in reviewing modern library resources, thanks are also due to Harrison Dekker, Business and Economics Information Specialist at the State Library of North Carolina in Raleigh. For permission to photograph parts of the university library, thanks to North Carolina State University in Raleigh and to Tracey Casorso, Director of the Friends of the Library. For help with several photographic illustrations, thanks to Yevonne Brannon, Kimberly Hale, Caroline Barbour, and Jean Funderburg of the Center for Urban Affairs and Community Services at the University and to Jeff Johnson of Johnson-Zabor & Associates, Inc., marketing research of the Research Triangle Park. And for his help with several graphic illustrations, thanks to my friend and colleague, Dan Norman. Finally, for many years of patient mentoring and support, I would like to thank my friend, John R. Griffin, former Senior Director of Marketing Services at Blue Cross and Blue Shield of North Carolina, where I spent eight years as Director of Marketing Research before opening my own business.

INTRODUCTION

This book is intended as a primer for small business owners and managers about methods in marketing research and competitive intelligence. It is intended for the busy manager, marketer, or customer service representative who simply does not have the time to spend weeks in the library looking through magazines and books for answers—or the money to hire a skilled professional researcher to conduct a survey.

GOING INTO BUSINESS

The world is changing. This book is very different from a book that might have been written on marketing research five years ago. Opportunities for entrepreneurs and small business owners have never been greater than today, but risks are also greater. Economic forces in the Western world are pushing trained and experienced workers out of their jobs in record numbers. Many of those individuals are trying to go into business for themselves. Most will fail. New technology is responsible for dispossessing many of these people of their jobs, but new technology is also creating new businesses and jobs.

Operating a business is certainly more complex today than it was a hundred years ago. We have a more complex tax and legal code to understand. International competition has crept into our local towns, and new technologies have transformed the way we do business. Markets are in constant turmoil. It is becoming harder to keep up with market developments. On the other hand, we have better sources of information for understanding our markets than ever before.

THE VALUE OF MARKETING RESEARCH

Time spent conducting marketing research generates no revenue for the firm. Therefore, it is sometimes thought to be unproductive time and is one of the first things to be cut when finances get tight. In the corporate world, reorganizations and budget cuts have squeezed market research out of many marketing and sales departments as corporate hierarchies have been flattened. Time has an opportunity cost—the revenues that might have been generated had that time been used for more rewarding activities—but not if that time is ill used.

Over the years, the value of time has constantly risen as the real per capita income of workers has increased. For the entrepreneur, however, the cost of time saved by not conducting marketing research will be too high if her knowledge is inaccurate or insufficient. Saving a week of research time is a poor economic decision if it encourages the use of 50 weeks a year trying to sell the wrong product to the wrong people at the wrong price.

The time and money spent doing marketing research before and after going into business is a superb investment if it produces *correct decisions* based on

- An accurate business plan
- An understanding of changes in the marketplace

LOW-COST, LEAST-TIME RESEARCH METHODS

Just as technology is changing the way we conduct business, it is also changing the options open to us for conducting marketing research. As a consequence, this book will consider the role of new technologies in lowering the cost of research and how the entrepreneur and small businessperson might take advantage of technology to reduce research costs and its time-burden.

The entrepreneur can minimize the direct and indirect costs of marketing research by

- Using secondary sources of information
- Using simple methods of gathering primary information
- Creating systems that ensure regular communication between customers and the firm

Together, these various tools should meet most of the information requirements of the business owner.

PLANNING TO SUCCEED

1

Entrepreneurs today face a tough time in developing a realistic business plan and then bringing their new businesses to profitability. The development of a realistic business plan presents even more of an obstacle than is generally recognized because many prospective entrepreneurs

- Do not really understand their markets
- Do not know their customers or their customers' wants
- Do not understand the reasons for their competitors' success
- Do not know how to price or promote their products or services

Yet these shortcomings do not stop us from trying to create our own businesses. Americans are certainly an action-oriented people. We have faith that hard work and determination will overcome all obstacles, and so we push ahead, confident that we can create a place for ourselves in the market.

Entrepreneurs use various methods to make important business decisions. Many copy their competitors (which just makes them indistinguishable from their competitors). Some sell the same product at a lower price. Others vary the product or service. Some try to target underserved groups only to learn that they are not truly underserved.

As a result, two out of three businesses allegedly fail during their first year, and four out of five fail within two years. They fail because they lack the financing required to stay the course until their fortunes turn upward. They fail because their owners lack the essential skills, personality, education, or business smarts needed to be in business at all. They fail because their owners don't know what they don't know. They fail, in short, because the business plan turns out to be

- An inaccurate or incomplete description of the market or the opportunities it presents
- A poor analysis of the products, services, pricing strategies, or promotional requirements for the market
- Based on an unrealistic expectation of the time it will take to bring the enterprise to profitability

This book is addressed to those who might, unknowingly, be in that failure-bound 80 percent. In it, we will talk frankly about how not having a firm knowledge of certain basic concepts and strategies will bring failure and how we can learn those things in the most economical and time-efficient way.

WHY ENTREPRENEURS DON'T PLAN

A very high proportion of business start-ups apparently begin without a business or marketing plan—good or bad. Amar Bhide, of the Harvard Business School, points out that comprehensive planning is not necessarily appropriate for many start-ups:

> However popular it may be in the corporate world, a comprehensive analytical approach to planning doesn't suit most start-ups. Entre-

preneurs typically lack the time and money to interview a representative cross section of potential customers, let alone analyze substitutes, reconstruct competitors' cost structures, or project alternative
technology scenarios. In fact, too much analysis can be harmful; by
the time an opportunity is investigated fully, it may not longer exist.
A city map and restaurant guide on a CD may be a winner in January
but worthless if delayed until December.[1]

Bhide is saying that, in some cases, too much time spent doing the
research might be better spent by getting the product to market.

In interviews with the founders of 100 of *Inc.* magazine's 1989
list of the 500 fastest-growing companies in the United States, Bhide
discovered that many of these entrepreneurs spent little effort on
their initial business plan:

- Forty-one percent had no business plan at all
- Twenty-six percent had just a rudimentary, back-of-the-
  envelope type of plan
- Only 5 percent worked up financial projections for investors
- Only 28 percent wrote up a full-blown business plan[2]

Some might interpret his results somewhat differently, however. The fact that these entrepreneurs tended to have rudimentary
plans does not mean that they did not do their marketing research.
The fact that the opportunities they pursued had a brief window
of opportunity merely implies that the methods they must have
had to use to identify opportunities, assess the market, and judge
their risks had to be time efficient. Whether they wrote down their
analysis and conclusions was far less important than the need to
act swiftly.

Others argue that writing down a plan is more an exercise of
self-discipline and providing documentation to obtain financing
than it is a necessity for a new business's success. And it's true that
writing down a plan does not guarantee that what is written down
is even close to being correct.

A plan based on weak data, poor market analysis, or incorrect assumptions will almost assuredly increase the chances of failure. It is this problem that marketing research is designed to correct. Moreover, doing without a written plan makes it almost impossible for your business advisors to review your assumptions, identified opportunities, and marketing program for errors.

WHY BUSINESSES FAIL

Businesses fail because what happens to them is not what their owners and managers thought was going to happen. In short, something was wrong with their understanding of the opportunities they perceived or with the way they pursued them. For example,

- They did not have enough capital to sustain themselves until their businesses became profitable
- Marketing efforts were ineffective or insufficient
- Management was ineffective.

Doubtless, some entrepreneurs fail because they put little trust in research and view it as nothing more than the accumulation of useless information. In fact, *business research is the organized effort to gather information relevant to the needs and problems of a business and should improve planning and decision making.* Money spent on the accumulation of such an information base is well spent if it leverages an organization into more sharply focused business strategies.

Any type of problem-solving activity involves a research process to gather information needed to analyze the issues and make a decision. How does one know what information to gather? The answer is to use the scientific method. One forms a hypothesis about the causes of a problem and then gathers information that enables one to determine whether the hypothesis is correct or not. We'll examine this process in more depth later.

THE ROLES OF MARKETING RESEARCH

This book is intended for entrepreneurs and small business managers who have had little, if any, training in how to conduct marketing research. Such individuals are also likely to have few trained employees to whom to assign this research. They have to market, manage, provide services to customers, keep records, and perform all the other activities that go into keeping a business afloat. As a result, time for marketing research tends to be squeezed out by all the time required for "essential" activities, and their marketing decisions become guesses or conclusions made on the basis of weak information. While those entrepreneurs are waiting to see whether they guessed correctly or not, their financial resources are being depleted. By the time they find they've guessed wrong, it's too late.

Entrepreneurs and small business managers might feel they can't spare the time to learn how to do and actually perform the research. Therefore, one emphasis of this volume is on teaching some basic techniques to lessen the time spent by the entrepreneur gathering information.

New and existing small businesses sometimes have another problem that limits the amount of marketing research they do: cash shortage and low profitability. Many of these businesses cannot afford professionally managed research projects. Therefore, a second emphasis of this book is on identifying ways to minimize the out-of-pocket expenses of marketing research—techniques that small business owners or managers can do themselves.

The role of marketing research for any size of enterprise is to provide the necessary information required by the marketing manager to make the correct marketing decisions for the firm. The term *marketing manager* refers to a role or set of roles within the firm. In the small firm, the entrepreneur or CEO him- or herself may fill all the roles of the marketing manager.

The Marketing Concept

The concept of the marketing manager was verbalized by J. B. McKitterick as early as 1957:

> The principal task of the marketing function in a management concept is not so much to be skillful in making the customer do what suits the interests of the business as to be skillful in conceiving and then making the business do what suits the interests of the customer.[3]

Thus, the marketing manager must know exactly what the customer wants and how to provide that better than competitors do.

The marketing concept is sometimes hard for entrepreneurs and some small business managers to accept. Small businesses are often started by *creative* or *technical* people—people with an idea, a dream, and specific types of expertise. Sometimes the dream is consistent with the market and will create or find its own market; sometimes it is inconsistent with the market and will be rejected. If the latter is the case, it seems preferable for the entrepreneur to modify her business a little so that it is consistent with the market than for the dream to die. America needs people with dreams and the drive to make them reality. Effective marketing research will provide the means for the entrepreneur to identify and make any needed modifications in her product or service and thus be received favorably by the marketplace.

The Uses of Marketing Research

The three major uses of marketing research are

- Marketing planning
- Marketing problem solving
- Control of the marketing process (monitoring)

Some of the major activities included within the scope of marketing research are listed in Table 1.1.[4] Some might add forecasting to this list; others might perhaps add some of the other activities of business research such as

- Acquisition studies
- Technology studies
- Location studies
- Cost studies
- Forecasting
- Operations research
- Personnel studies

A review of the activities in Table 1.1 should convince the entrepreneur or small business manager that he already does at least some marketing research, which often goes under the guise of sales or marketing management.

TABLE 1.1 Scope of activities in marketing research

Research focus	Types of research
Advertising research	Media selection
	Advertising copy development
	Customer motivation research
Product research	Packaging decisions research
	New product development research
	Competitor product studies
Sales and market research	Estimating the size of a market
	Market share analysis
	Market profiles and descriptions
	Setting sales quotas
	Sales analysis
	Analysis of product distribution channels
	Studies of promotional tactics
	Store audits

Most of the time, marketing issues are framed as questions from a marketing decision maker—questions such as those displayed in Table 1.2.

TABLE 1.2   The roles of marketing research

Use of data	Questions
Planning	**Define the market in which the business is involved.**
	How large is this market?
	What are the basic trends in the domestic economy? How will these trends affect the market for our products?
	What is our share of this market?
	Is this market growing, mature, or declining in size?
	What changes can we expect in customer purchasing patterns? Are these due to changes in real income, tastes and values, or in the mix of customers in the market?
	What are our competitors' market shares, and how are those changing?
	What new markets are evolving? What products and services will be needed to serve them? Should we enter these new markets? How can we take advantage of those new markets?
	What changes will be needed in our distribution strategies and sales force over the next five years?
	How do we compare in customer service and satisfaction with our primary competitors?
Problem Solving	**Problem-solving research focuses on identifying the causes of marketing problems as functions of a poorly planned marketing mix.**
1. Product	Which of several alternative product/service designs are most likely to be successful?

TABLE 1.2 *Continued*

Use of data	Questions
	What is the reason for poor sales performance? The product? Service? Support after the sale?
	What action should we take to counter a new product/service being introduced by our competitors?
2. Price	How should we price our new products or services? Are our prices high or low compared to those of our primary competition?
3. Place	What should be our discount for consignment sales?
	What types of intermediate dealers, agents, brokers, etc., should be used?
	What levels of discounts or commissions should we pay?
4. Promotion	What should the total promotion budget be, and how do we allocate it among competing uses?
	What specific product features and benefits should we use in our promotions?
	Which media are most suitable for our products and services?
	How effective have our previous promotions been?
Control	**What are our market shares by area, product line, and customer category?**
	Are we covering our various target market areas as well as we should?
	What is our business's image among the various markets we serve, and how is our image changing?

Adapted from Gilbert A. Churchill Jr., *Marketing Research: Methodological Foundations*, 3rd ed. (New York: The Dryden Press, 1983), 10. Churchill's table was itself adapted from James H. Myers and Richard R. Mead, "The Management of Marketing Research," 23–46. Copyright 1969 by Intext, Inc., New York.

EFFECTS OF ENVIRONMENTAL FACTORS

In addition to examining business decisions, marketing research can also be used to conduct analyses of factors such as the following:

- The political and legal environment
- Competitors and the technological environment
- The national and international economy
- The cultural and social environment[5]

Of course, these environmental factors are not controllable by the business manager, but information from each of these domains is important for a variety of reasons, such as

- Complying with the law and the values of the community
- Adjusting plans as interest rates, unemployment, and economic activity waxes and wanes
- Responding to the actions of competitors
- Adjusting to changes in public attitudes, tastes, and wants

These topics, too, come within the purview of marketing research. Therefore, later in this book some discussion is devoted to staying informed about the community, the economy, and the competition.

THE MARKETING MIX

The controllable factors of the marketing mix (Figure 1.1) are

- The product or service offered
- The price charged for the product(s) or service(s)
- The promotional techniques used to communicate with the marketplace
- The means for distributing the product or service to the market (or providing place utility)

10

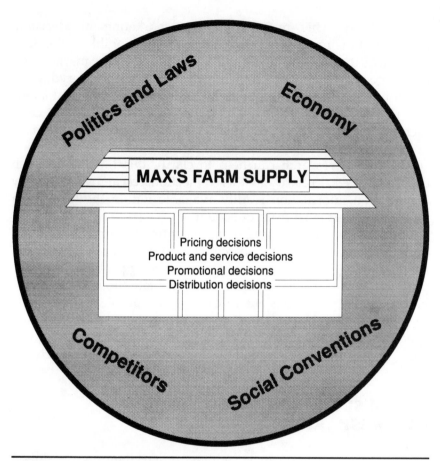

FIGURE 1.1   The Marketing Mix

Information about decisions that affect the marketing mix is essential in examining *cause-and-effect relationships* between a firm's action and the market's reaction. When a business makes a decision on pricing policy, to introduce a new product, to sponsor an advertising campaign, or to distribute products in a certain way, there will be a response by the market to those decisions.

Obviously, when managers make a marketing mix decision, they expect the results of their decision to be favorable to the firm. Sometimes they are mistaken, and the response by the marketplace is unexpectedly negative. In the hustle and bustle of everyday decision making, the connection between a past decision and a current market response gets lost, and decision makers simply can't identify which of their past decisions is responsible for what is going wrong today.

Marketing research can help to clarify this linkage between cause and effect. In clarifying this connection, research analysts rely as much on information readily available within the firm as on information retrieved from outside it.

In designing a marketing plan, the entrepreneur tries to determine through marketing research and experience just how to set her marketing mix. In researching a marketing problem with any product or service, the manager must evaluate the role of each of her marketing mix decisions in causing the problem. And in researching the use by customers of her product or service, the manager must develop means for collecting information on an ongoing basis, managing that data, and arranging it into useful reports.

CAN BUSINESSPEOPLE DO THEIR OWN RESEARCH?

One might as well ask, can entrepreneurs start their own business? They can, but they may not always succeed. They may not succeed when they try to do their own marketing research, either. Just as when marketing specialized products or services, doing marketing research often involves experimentation and trying unfamiliar techniques. But as long as a road map is available, most who try can muddle through—and in the doing, learn how to do it better next time. Even marketing research professionals accept that they will make mistakes and learn from them. That is a good attitude to take into any undertaking.

KNOWING YOUR MARKET AND YOUR COMPETITION | **2**

Any businessperson has got to know who his customers are and what they want, who his competitors are, and what kind of offer will persuade each customer to buy from him rather than his competitors. Gaining this information is what marketing research and competitive intelligence is all about. If you don't know these things, you will not be in business for long. But few of us start out knowing nothing about these factors. Your need to do marketing research will depend on what you know when you start.

Suppose, however, that someone wants to start a business and doesn't know any of those things.

- If she doesn't research who her customers are, she will not know whom to prospect and will waste time and resources marketing to the wrong people.
- If she doesn't research what her prospective buyers want, her product or service offering is likely to be a mismatch with those wants, and her prospects will pass over her offer.

- If she doesn't research what her competitors are offering to her customers, then she loses an opportunity to identify at a very low cost what she must do to keep her customers.
- If her prospects are already doing business with her competitors and she doesn't research that relationship, she loses the opportunity to identify what the customer has at least found to be an acceptable offer.
- If she doesn't monitor her prospects' satisfaction with the products and service provided by her competitors, she misses the opportunity to discover whether she can take those customers away from her competitors. With that information, she knows not to waste her time and money prospecting those customers until the situation changes.

Investing a little time and a few dollars in marketing research can save months of casting around and wasting money keeping a business going in the wrong direction. The out-of-pocket cost of doing or buying marketing research is trivial next to those costs. The entrepreneur who fails to gather this information and perform the analysis is operating blindly. The end result will very probably be squandered resources, broken dreams, and business failure.

THE IMPORTANCE OF MARKETING GOALS

If you have clear marketing goals, you are halfway to identifying what you need to know. But goal setting is easier when you already know how you are doing. Once you know where the opportunities are, what your performance is in pursuing those opportunities, and why you are achieving what you are achieving, you can set realistic goals.

But for many entrepreneurs starting out, it is not so clear where the opportunities are, because they have no record of achievement or basis for determining those things. Many of these beginners enter a try-and-fail cycle for a while, attempting to find a niche where they can survive. Some never find a profitable niche and quit. They may not lose money, but neither do they make any.

In this situation, setting realistic goals is much harder. Such entrepreneurs may never find the proper focus for their efforts and end by putting out feelers in all directions at once, hoping that one will survive and thrive.

For some, the issue of the service or product to be offered is easier to pin down. Each year, thousands of individuals are pushed out of jobs in corporate downsizings. Others choose to leave, taking with them ideas, technology, contacts, and contracts. For those with the skills needed in the expanding industries, there are opportunities in entrepreneurship. Some of those individuals go into business for themselves, providing almost exactly the same services they provided for their previous employers. Obviously, such people don't start from scratch. Much of their "research" on their market of interest has already been done over the years.

Some entrepreneurs start without a real idea of how to develop a realistic marketing plan. After all, entrepreneurs are not all marketers. Many a creative writer has started a magazine or newsletter without a market study. Software developers sometimes begin developing a program idea without a clear idea of who will want it. Many a consultant has taken his skills and worked into a market by finding a need through trial and error. So long as the skills, methods, or technologies are not obsolete, success is possible. The cost, of course, is the time and money spent searching for a service or product and a market until the focus emerges.

In a crowded market, understanding your customer's needs and your competitors is even more imperative. The margin of error is narrower. You have to make fewer mistakes because mistakes drive up your direct and indirect costs. Marketing research lowers your costs of doing business by reducing the mistakes you make—by increasing the quantity and quality of information available to you for making business decisions.

Using Marketing Research to Find the Easiest Path

Moving into a market niche where there are no competitors is the ideal marketing strategy. You provide a product or service that buyers want, and your prospective customers are underserved, so you have a clear field. Theoretically, all you have to do is make calls and take orders. But how many of us have such a clear field? And when might such a situation occur?

Well, you might own a patent for a new technology that could displace existing technologies in the marketplace. With this technology, you can take business away from competitors who are still utilizing the older technology by offering a superior product at a lower price.

Maybe you are fortunate enough to find an unmet need in a local personal service field. This may be because of unaggressive competitors who have not really had to work hard to do well, leading to some discontent among customers about service, price, or the quality of the product or services they are buying. This happenstance provides an opportunity for the entrepreneur to innovate as well. By providing faster, lower-cost, and superior service, you might take market share away from your competitors.

But if you are a middle-aged music teacher who researches the market and finds an opportunity to repair automobiles, how suited are you to take advantage of that opportunity? The marketing concept that tells us to find what the market wants and provide it is not necessarily going to work *at the individual level*. No one is guaranteed to find an opportunity to work in any particular field. The market is a harsher place than that.

Marketing Research after Start-Up

After start-up comes a whole series of marketing questions for which an owner or manager may not have the answers, for example:

- What are the most effective techniques you could use to win new clients?
- How should you prospect?
- How do you write an effective sales letter?
- Exactly how should you promote your business through advertising and public relations?
- Specifically, what incentives will you need to cut into your competitors' business? (Examples, guarantees, promotions, gifts, price cuts, etc.)
- What will be the responses of your competitors to your efforts to take business away from them, and how should you respond to them?

Finding the answers to these kinds of operational questions can also be the job of marketing research.

Marketing Research When Competition Is Intense

Suppose you are not able to identify a gap that you feel is consistent with your strengths and simply go into business anyway. Chances are you will find yourself in a marketplace populated by aggressive competitors and satisfied customers. Especially if you are tackling competitors head-on in a start-up, there is no substitute for understanding your competitors' strengths and weaknesses and aggressively using that information to survive. By knowing how your competitors' customers feel about the service, price, and products being provided by your competitors, you will at least know what relationship and offer you have to better.

In intensely competitive markets, you may also experience frequent marketing problems. Marketing research also possesses a battery of tools for problem solving. You might consider surveys, field interviews and focus groups as techniques for understanding the causes of poor sales, low customer retention, and low repeat business.

Marketing Research in a Growing or Mature Market

If your small business is past the start-up stage in a growing market, failure to pursue a growth strategy means allowing competitors to grow stronger. Your share of the market will decline. Your customers will observe the growth of your competitors and may question the quality of your management, product, or service.

This perception will create a weakness that your competitors can exploit. Marketing research in such an environment can be used to track market shares, to monitor the introduction of competitors' new products, and to research customers' acceptance of your own new products.

If your business is in a mature or declining industry, the wisest strategy is sometimes to focus on retaining your existing customers. This means concentrating your sales efforts and customer service on the customers you have and putting less emphasis on prospecting for new business. Marketing research in a mature or declining industry is commonly focused on monitoring customer satisfaction and identifying competitor inroads into your market share.

WHAT ARE YOUR RESEARCH GOALS?

The status of a business—whether it is just in the planning stage, in start-up, or has been in existence for a while—will make a great deal of difference for the goals and character of any marketing research performed.

If you are a wise entrepreneur, you will make your planning decisions in the context of your own strengths, interests, professional background, and life experiences. It will pay you to *do research on yourself*. You might start with a self-assessment and then proceed to marketing and business research based on the answers. A good many books on starting a small business ignore the relationship between the entrepreneur's interests and experience and the choice of business. That is unfortunate, because enduring the frustration and privations of most start-ups is possible only when the entrepreneur possesses the enthusiasm of a true believer. So the first question of your self-assessment might be

---

1. What are my own personal strengths and weaknesses, and what are the implications of those strengths and weaknesses for the type of business activity I should consider? For example, am I good at prospecting and dealing with customers, or am I happier working alone? Am I creatively oriented, or am I technically oriented?

A friend of mine, Dr. Walton Jones, Professor Emeritus of the University of North Carolina, has spent many years developing programs that train and support new entrepreneurs. He advises that to be successful in a new business, you need to do three things:

- Choose a business that is right for you. If you don't like what you are doing, you'll never survive the first years.
- Choose a business idea based on your experience and expertise. Build on your strengths and background. Make sure you truly believe in it, or you will never be able to sell it to anyone else.
- Study the market. Find out if your idea meets a genuine need better than anyone else's.

Dr. Jones feels that the prospective entrepreneur should start by doing research on herself to determine whether she has the personal strengths needed to endure a business start-up.

---

2. What businesses, products, and markets do you know the most about?

Too often, individuals go into an off-the-shelf business with no relationship to their past education or employment. Your education and experience represent your key business strengths. You have, in effect, already done a lot of marketing research on those areas, and you probably already know where to find much of the data needed to write your marketing plan. Consider those strengths seriously when deciding what venture to undertake.

---

3. What customers (individuals or businesses) would be logical targets given your strengths, interests, background, and experience?

Here, for the first time, we are beginning to get into issues that are traditionally covered in a marketing plan. Ask yourself questions about the characteristics of markets, customers, and wants:

- Do you understand the problems or wants of your customers?
- Do you understand their business and point of view?
- How large are your potential markets in terms of numbers of customers, units of product sold per year, dollar volume, or other measurements?
- How fast is your market growing? Is it mature or declining?
- Which subgroups (segments) in that market are you best equipped to serve?
- How large are each of these segments in terms of people, units, dollar volume, or other measurements?

---

4. Over what marketing area will I operate my business?

This area might be a five-mile radius for a retail store or all of North America and Europe for a mail-order business. The larger the market, the greater the possibility of finding underserved market segments within that area, but distant markets are more expensive to service. Consider these issues in defining your feasible marketing area.

You might also consider asking these questions:

- How do my competitors define their market areas?
- Where can I find a source of data that will allow me to answer all the subquestions under Question 3 for my defined geographic area? There are usually sources available from secondary sources, which we will discuss in later chapters.

> 5. Within the geographic market and product/service categories you have initially defined, what needs are not served or are underserved among the customers you feel that you could serve?

How will you identify these unmet needs? Because the market is constantly changing, you might need to consider collecting primary information on customer needs.

> 6. What do these customers want from suppliers, and how do they buy?

Buyers of cold drinks might want convenience and taste and buy on impulse with little forethought. Buyers of new automobiles, on the other hand, may be influenced by self-image, engineering quality, price, and features but spend many months looking and comparing. Will you have to bid on contracts, or can you simply set prices? Will you customarily have to negotiate contracts? How people buy will make a great deal of difference in how you must conduct the marketing function.

> 7. How can you distribute your products or services in a cost-efficient manner? Can you provide service after the sale in the same way?

If you are in a mail-order business, then you can mail or ship the product to your customer. But if you are a consultant, a sales trainer, a plumber, or a manufacturer, you will have to consider the issue of cost-efficient distribution. How exactly will you prospect for business? Why is that the best way for your particular business? What service is likely to be required after the sale? And how will you provide it?

> 8. Which firms operating within your selected marketing area are providing competing products or services to your prospective customers?

How will you identify your competitors? Are lists available?

> 9. What are the strengths and weaknesses of those competitors?

Profile their marketing mixes and strategies. How do they do things? What makes their market positions strong or weak? What makes them vulnerable to your marketing efforts?

> 10. If my potential customers are already purchasing my selected product or service from my competitors, why?

If they are purchasing from your competitors, how satisfied are they with

- The price they are paying?
- The product or service features they are getting?
- The way the product or service is delivered?
- The way their account is serviced?

Do you know what your competitors are doing right? What could you do better, cheaper, faster, or more conveniently?

- How much better, cheaper, faster, or more conveniently would you have to be to tempt them to deal with you?

These ten questions are offered as an initial set of prospective research goals. Questions 1 and 2 are preliminary to preparing a marketing plan. They suggest how you might begin to define your own business.

Many entrepreneurs have found that it is only too easy to write down a schedule for their marketing activities that has no relation to what is realistic or effective. So I am going to suggest several additional research goals that relate to discovering effective ways to prospect and target your marketing efforts:

---

11. In your chosen business, what methods have been proven to be most successful in identifying prospective customers?

Can you find business lists containing the right businesses and individuals within those businesses? Will lists of names be available through some community business organization such as the chamber of commerce? Or will you have to call every business and play telephone networking?

> 12. In your chosen business, what steps will be most effective for promoting your business, becoming known and accepted by your target market, and gaining access to decision makers?

Is print, radio, or television advertising a viable method to announce your business or offer to the business community? For some products, they may be; for many others, they may not. Should you launch a publicity campaign? Give speeches in the community? Write letters to the editor? What works and does not work in your industry or businesses?

> 13. In your chosen business, how long should you expect to spend cultivating customers before securing an order or contract?

In some businesses, customers must be courted for months before the opportunity arises to make a presentation. In others, a sale comes soon after a prospect reads your advertisement. You need to find out what to expect for your particular type of business.

> 14. In your chosen business, what sales incentives are customary or understood?

Will the customer expect periodic price reduction incentives, price guarantees, return privileges, free service with the sale, free telephone consultation, and so on? In any business, time and tradition tend to institutionalize certain trade practices that customers come to expect. If you do not know about those practices, they will trip you up.

15. In your chosen industry and business, how critical will the regular introduction of new products or services be to continued success? How will you create the capacity to develop and/or introduce new products to your markets?

Plan on monitoring industry trade journals, attending trade shows, and tracking new product introductions by your competition. All of these activities come under the heading of marketing research. If you find you need to assign new product development to special departments within your firm, how will you integrate your marketing research efforts with those in-house resources?

16. Will you need an advertising or public relations program?

• How will you develop the advertising concept?
• How will you test the concept before rollout?
• How will you evaluate the advertising program once it is under way?

IDENTIFY POTENTIAL BUSINESS ADVISORS

Whether you are considering a start-up or are already in business and simply wish to do a better job in your market planning, developing a network of business advisors will prove to be an important step. If well chosen, these individuals can not only help you make wiser decisions once you are in business but will also be able to suggest

- Refinements of your research goals
- Where you might find information
- How to go about retrieving it
- What some of the answers might be

Having a professional marketing research advisor and/or an information broker in your advisory group may enable you to identify specific sources of industry data, survey reports, government or university studies, and many secondary sources of information on your industry. Having a professional sales representative on your advisory group will provide priceless practical information on the most effective ways to prospect, keep records, set goals, and evaluate performance. Having a librarian on your advisory group pretty well puts a library in your back pocket and gives you a staff member to look for information needed in your marketing plan when you are busy elsewhere.

It will be worth your time to actually pay these individuals to attend a regular meeting to provide feedback for your planning and marketing efforts. Other wise choices for your panel of business advisors might be a college business professor, a CPA, or an executive with your chamber of commerce—how much might these individuals be worth to you in saved time and wasted resources?

Low-cost marketing research does not necessarily mean cost-*free* marketing research. There is no point in doing poor research. And if you are not a professional marketer or marketing researcher, you may not recognize an incomplete analysis or error when you make it. Especially if your business is a one-person operation, one of the scarcest resources you are likely to have as an entrepreneur is time.

If a monthly meeting costs you $200 to pull together and conduct, how much do you value the time you will need to identify the sources of information you need, search for them, retrieve them, and then read them? After reading the material you find, you will need to spend time synthesizing it and writing it into your marketing plan. If your research is incomplete or in error, who is available to you to spot the errors and redirect your efforts to strengthen your plan?

I suggest that these activities may well take you weeks to accomplish—time during which you could be implementing your marketing plans, time during which you could be prospecting, time during which you could be generating income with which to pay your bills.

Do the research but also provide yourself with a resource that can strengthen your work.

CREATIVE RESEARCH PLANNING

3

In chapter 2, we spent considerable time discussing basic marketing research goals. These will cover much of the information needed by the individual who is thinking about going into business or who is preparing her own marketing plan. The manager of an existing small business may select different goals, for example, ones related to marketing planning, solving specific marketing problems, or maintaining control of marketing efforts through various monitoring techniques.

Let's consider the prospective or new entrepreneur first. The small business manager may, of course, wish to reconsider elements of her own past marketing plan, so many of the new entrepreneur's goals may be relevant for her as well.

The setting of goals is the first stage of your plan to do your own marketing research. For each of the research goals you set for yourself, do the following:

- Define the information needed to reach your goal
- Determine where the information is
- Identify the most cost- and time-efficient way to retrieve that information at that location
- Decide how you will process the information

It might be helpful to create a worksheet something like the one displayed in Table 3.1. If necessary, consider an 8" x 14" or 8" x 17" sheet of paper—or even two 8" x 11" pages taped together—to give yourself large enough columns to write in your answers. The headings in this table comprise the essential elements of your research design. Whenever you set out to do some marketing research, consider creating a table like this one to plan your work.

In Table 3.1, the first two questions from chapter 2 have been entered as well as some steps for dealing with them. These steps are only suggestions; feel free to add your own. There are probably many suitable approaches for dealing with these questions—most of which will lead to the same conclusions.

DEFINING THE INFORMATION YOU NEED

Needing to make a decision about marketing direction or problems will not necessarily mean that you know what information you need. But as you begin thinking about what you would want to understand before making a decision, you can work your way to defining your information needs. Gilbert A. Churchill, in his excellent text *Marketing Research: Methodological Foundations*, makes the distinction between *decision problems* and *research problems*.

A decision problem involves deciding what needs to be done about a marketing problem. Even apparently straightforward decision problems can create very complex research problems, which involve determining what information will be needed to solve that decision problem.

TABLE 3.1 Research planning worksheet

Question #	Research goals	What information is needed?	Where is the information?	How will I search for this information?	How will I retrieve the information?	How will I process this information?
1.	What are my own personal strengths and weaknesses, and what are the implications of those strengths and weaknesses for the type of business activity I should consider?	Objective info on my own personal strengths and weaknesses. Educational specialties. Past performance on the job. Inventory of personal characteristics needed by entrepreneurs.	In myself. In friends and business associates. In educational and employment records. Employee performance reviews Local small business centers, SCORE, and entrepreneurial training courses. In literature on the entrepreneurial character.	Self-diagnosis. Arrange interviews with people who know me well. Research character traits of entrepreneurs and successful small business owners.	Self-assessment tests. Occupational interest and skills inventories. Conduct interviews with business advisors. Examine past performance reviews. Read materials on the entrepreneurial character.	I will summarize the information retrieved and present my conclusions to family and business advisors.

2.	What businesses, products, or markets do you know the most about? What are the technical skills I developed on the job?	Past employment or any special industry training programs. Personal files, training materials, reports, etc., about those industries.	Review those industry materials. Conduct a personal skills inventory.	I will write a personal capability statement. I will present this capability statement to my business advisory group.

Defining the Problem

The marketing researcher must make sure that she understands the real decision problem—not necessarily the problem defined by a decision maker. The following scenario shows how important this is.

The owner of a small shoe business specializing in orthopedic shoes has become dissatisfied with the mail-order response to a long-running classified ad in his market area. Until a year ago, sales were trending upward, but since then they have leveled off and actually began declining about six months ago.

About a third of his sales for the shoes occur in the store; the remainder are mail-order sales and phone-in orders. The store's mail-order business has been mostly repeat sales to established customers who reside at a distance from the store.

The store's business manager suggests a modification in the ad copy to reverse the declining response rates and asks his marketing manager for his reaction. The decision problem, as the business manager sees it, is whether to change the ad copy or not.

One possible course of action by the marketing manager would be simply to rewrite the copy, run the revised ad in the regular media for a month, and see if sales increase as expected. The question is, however, whether the research problem is how to revise the ad and measure the outcome of the test or whether it is something else entirely.

Redefining the Problem

Our marketing manager might not accept the alternatives presented to him by the business manager and might instead try to frame his research goal so as to make sure sure that the decision problem has been correctly defined. For example, he might ask, "Who has been buying from us in the past and why?"

When he analyzes the store's internal sales records, he discovers that two-thirds of its recent mail-order sales have been in remote rural areas and that it has been these sales to rural residents that have been declining. Storefront business has in fact been growing.

So, he asks, what exactly is causing our sales in rural areas to decline? Is it competition? Could it be declining demand by our customers? Or could it have something to do with where and how often our ad is appearing?

Suppose neither manager knows that circulation of the newspaper in which the ad has been running has been steadily eroding in rural areas due to rising distribution costs, price increases, and competition from other local newspapers. The marketing manager discovers this by requesting subscription data by county from the newspaper normally used for his ads. He beings to wonder if the problem in his rural markets is due to the declining circulation of his selected advertising medium.

Now he can focus his research efforts on those rural areas to find out why the ad is being less effective. He might recommend testing the existing ad in other newspapers that are gaining circulation in those areas. He might also suggest a survey of past customers in rural areas who have not repeated purchases in the last two years to find out where they are replacing their worn-out shoes. Or he might telephone shoe stores in those areas (using telephone books available at local libraries) to determine whether they might be stocking or fitting people for orthopedic shoes and thus drawing customers away from his direct sales program.

So the problem may be the ad's draw, or it may be that other factors are influencing the ad's performance. It is the job of the marketing researcher to be flexible enough in his thinking to recognize the potential causes and then decide what kind of information is needed to evaluate them.

How does our marketing researcher know to look at these other possibilities? Rather than just accepting his boss's opinion as his guide, he defines his research problem in terms of a series of questions that force him to consider and check all possible explanations:

What alternative reasons might account for the decline in response rates?

What share of the declines in response rates can be attributed to environmental factors, such as competition, migration of population, changes in government regulation or program aid, and so on?

How can I evaluate the effectiveness of the current ad's copy separately from those other factors?

Will copy modifications alone improve response?

What kind of data will I require to perform an analysis?

The Costs of Not Doing the Research

If the marketing manager is also the researcher, as is the case in the shoe store, then he must avoid jumping to conclusions and think through all the feasible causes of the marketing problem. That is hard to do. Sometimes easy-to-get information points to one explanation, while hard-to-find information reveals others. But generally, the costs associated with implementing an incorrect marketing strategy are far higher to the firm than the costs of conducting research that would have revealed the correct strategies. Incorrect decisions are expensive, and the longer those incorrect strategies are pursued, the greater the cost to the firm.

Research goals must recognize not only the possible explanations behind a decision goal but also where the information is to be found and in which form it will be of value. In our example, quantitative circulation figures arranged by county were acquired from the relevant newspapers. Are the shoe store's internal sales records similarly computerized and organized so that annual sales of specific types of shoes can be reported by zip code or county?

Have lists of past customers been maintained that might support a survey of those customers?

DETERMINE WHERE THE INFORMATION IS

As the previous example illustrates, important information for your research projects may exist in the minds of managers and employees, in company records, in outside organizations (such as newspaper circulation records or rural shoe stores), or in the behavior of customers. It may also exist at the local library, chamber of commerce, competitor operations, government repositories or offices, or at university libraries. Many of these can be classified as *secondary sources* because the information already exists. The problem is to find where. *Primary data* is new information that you must develop from scratch, as from a special market survey.

American society is awash in data. There is so much of it that just storing and organizing it is a major industry in itself. The U.S. Census creates vast amounts of data on the environment through its decennial census, *Current Population Surveys, Establishment Surveys,* tax report records, and other projects. Throughout the United States, many university libraries have been designated as government document repositories.

For the average businessperson, finding information throughout the country is a daunting task, but the key secondary sources of information will always include the following:

Libraries and resource centers throughout the world

Competitors

Convenient information vehicles such as telephone books and key newspapers and magazines

Commercial databases

Customers and prospective customers

Internal company records

You will find that many sources exist for part or all of your information requirements, but each one will have different direct and indirect costs associated with it—in terms of both money and time. In many instances, you will not be able to determine whether particular information is of value until you have it in hand, which may mean having to pay a fee or spending a day traveling to examine it. It therefore pays to determine the content of the information before you spend either money or time on accessing it. This, too, is a part of the research process.

Associated with this question of how best to access information is your choice of research design. There are three major categories of research design: (1) *exploratory research*, (2) *descriptive studies*, and (3) *causal research designs*.[1]

Exploratory Research

The major emphasis in exploratory research is on the discovery of ideas and insights. A decision problem characterized as being due to declining sales might, in fact, be due to many causes. Exploratory research that helps to identify each of those contributing causes permits further research efforts to examine each of those causes separately.

Exploratory research is also very helpful in initiating a study because it helps the analyst to understand all aspects of a problem or subject. *Searches of the literature* are a form of exploratory research that concentrates on secondary data sources. *Focus groups*, a form of group interviewing, are another excellent exploratory primary data collection method.

Experience surveys are also a productive way to perform exploratory research. They are very common in business and are often conducted by people who do not consider what they are doing as research at all. In experience surveys, individuals with recognized expertise in a subject of interest are surveyed or interviewed to document their views on the subject matter at hand.

Case studies represent yet another way to conduct exploratory research on a subject or problem. To understand the causes of declining sales throughout a market area, an investigator might intensively study the actions and results of a salesperson in a rural area and of another in a major city.

In case studies, the investigator attempts to understand what is happening and why. Any previously formed theories are put aside in an effort to understand what those involved in the situation or activity under study believe the problem to be.

Descriptive Studies

Unlike exploratory research, descriptive studies are rigidly prescribed by the researcher's hypothesis about the subject or problem under study. In addition, descriptive research also requires decisions on technical issues such as the following:

- Who or what will be measured?
- When will the measurements be taken?
- Where will the measurements be taken?
- Why are we measuring them, and why are we doing it in one way instead of another?
- How shall we measure them?

Descriptive studies often involve the collection of structured statistical data that can be verified with statistical testing techniques. Typically, these methods employ either cross-sectional (all records cover the same calendar dates) or longitudinal (time series) data and present various potential statistical problems. However, much can be accomplished using relatively simple methods such as tables, cross-tabs, and simple graphics to understand problems of interest.

Causal Research Designs

Causal research is concerned with understanding the connection between cause and effect, which means that most causal research designs are experiments. Although business managers can certainly conduct experiments in the course of their marketing efforts, they cannot generally control or eliminate all the factors that might influence the final results. Causal research is therefore best performed in an isolated, controlled environment such as a laboratory. These methods tend to utilize highly trained research specialists, take considerable time to plan and implement, and cost more than you and I would want to spend. Because of these considerations, we will not consider causal research methods any further.

CARRY OUT YOUR SEARCH

Secondary data is unlikely to meet all of the information requirements for most research projects. Even after the most thorough search, you may still find that the completeness of the data collected is wanting, its relevance is marginal, or its contents are dated. If so, you will have to consider primary data collection—perhaps a survey of the marketplace. Some primary data collection methods are covered in later chapters.

DECIDE THE MOST COST- AND TIME-EFFICIENT WAY TO RETRIEVE YOUR INFORMATION

Simply because you've located information that you believe may be of value in completing a research goal does not necessarily mean that you have it in hand. You may know, for example, that a potentially important document about your chosen market is available in San Francisco, but if you are in Trenton, New Jersey, that article may not do you much good.

Consider for a moment how you could access that clipping. The telephone is one of the most inexpensive tools for obtaining information. Is the document short enough that it can be faxed to you? If not, can it be scanned into a computer and "modemed" to you?

Longer documents can be sent by regular or express mail. If there is a charge to see the information, check with reference librarians to see whether the same document can be found in a library nearby. In many instances, documents are stored electronically, and you can view them on-line—possibly even from your home or office personal computer. Also, check on the companies that work with libraries to find and photocopy documents for a modest fee. Your reference librarian can show you how to place an order, and you will have your document within an hour or two.

Primary data can also be acquired more efficiently with the aid of technological tools, but there is no real substitute for the tried-and-true methods of primary data collection. Interviews, surveys, and observation are still required to collect the desired data, but they can often be accomplished through telephones, faxes, and on-line news groups these days.

DECIDE HOW YOU WILL PROCESS YOUR INFORMATION

Analysis of information is usually a process of logical examination. *Marketing planning*, for example, uses information primarily to describe the marketplace, including its problems and opportunities, and to detail how the business will act to take advantage of those opportunities or deal with those problems.

In *problem-solving research*, researchers retrieve data about alternative causes and solutions to marketing problems.

Marketing information systems involve the selection of an information requirements model to monitor the marketplace and to support relationship marketing strategies. For these systems, marketers and researchers define their long-term marketing information needs and collect similar data over long periods of time. Database marketers enhance these systems by overlaying purchased data on these records to influence the buying decisions of customers and prospects.

Marketing Planning

Most businesses generally prepare an annual marketing plan. Marketing research for such plans is generally of a descriptive character. Marketers may need to perform some degree of analysis on this information, but there is usually no need for creating complex research designs or databases, performing statistical tests or estimates, and so forth. Processing this type of collected information therefore generally involves a written description of markets, customers, competitors, niche, and strategies.

Monitoring Markets

Monitoring is an especially useful technique for small businesses for a variety of reasons. Monitoring activities generate a consistent database of information about the environment, customers, prospects, and competitors over an extended period of time. These databases provide a rich source of data for analysis, comparisons, and management reporting. Monitoring can be used to describe customers, prospects, and competitors and, consequently, to update your marketing plan. It can be used in many cases for analysis of marketing problems (as for the direct marketer of orthopedic shoes in the previous example). Or it can be used for database marketing, tickler systems (sales databases used to periodically reprospect potential customers), sales performance reviews, and many other purposes.

Problem-Solving Research

Problem-solving research is a third major focus of marketing research. Marketing research performed for problem-solving must

- Include inquiries about all the feasible alternative causes of the defined problem
- Take measurements that permit meaningful evaluation of each alternative cause of the defined problem
- Enable decision makers to identify one or more appropriate courses of action to eliminate the problem

In a sense, every instance of problem-solving research is unique. It usually involves collecting primary data because of the need to customize the data collected to the problem. It may also be the most expensive option, but it may be unavoidable. If a marketing problem emerges that is serious enough to assign to a marketing research analyst, the costs of allowing the status quo to continue far outweigh the costs of the research.

Readers should be aware that this form of research is also the "meat and potatoes" of the commercial research industry. Most of the research that takes place within the industry of professional marketing researchers is probably of this type. There is no need to assume, however, that the average businessperson cannot perform this type of research. To provide the tools for such eventualities, this book contains chapters on such primary data collection methods as personal interviews, focus groups, and random surveys as well as a chapter about problem-solving marketing research.

WORK YOUR PLAN

Now that you've thought through your research goals, identified your data requirements, chosen how best to search for that data, and decided how to implement your search, it is time to get to work. Try to set aside time to conduct your research each week and keep your findings on file. Remember, you will be using this information to produce tangible products. For the entrepreneur, this information will go into a written marketing plan. For the small business manager, the information may be used to

- Update a marketing plan
- Set in place a marketing information system or other customer- or market-monitoring process
- Identify solutions to persistent marketing problems

Each of these uses are covered later in this book. However, the next three chapters deal with how to find and access research data.

CONVENIENT SOURCES FOR MARKETING RESEARCH

4

As a busy businessperson, you probably have a need for several convenient means to monitor your community and marketplace—probably on a daily basis. Fortunately, newspapers, radios, televisions, and telephone books are close at hand, and these can be among the most handy resources for systematic marketing research. Each day soon after arising, I read my daily paper. I listen to the radio in my car and sometimes watch television in the evening. And I can't think of a day I haven't had occasion to reference my local telephone book for business or research.

SELECTING PRINT AND ELECTRONIC MEDIA TO MONITOR

The Local Business Press

For many small businesses, the local area is the primary marketing battleground. Most likely, your success and that of your competitors is mirrored in local newspapers, radio, television, and other communications media.

Local also can mean the city or area in which your competitors are located, if not where you are. For example, I live in North Carolina, but many of my strongest competitors have their headquarters in New York City, Boston, or Chicago. To do marketing research on those competitors, I might want to check the major papers in those cities.

In addition to providing an inexpensive source of data, these media should be considered for advertising or press releases about your own business. The media, after all, are a major resource for communicating with the public. Even the smallest business should have a communication strategy described in its marketing plan. Use of these media for marketing research simply reflects the use of them as advertising and public relations tools.

The local business press will also include much general information about the business community, political events and legislative analysis, government economic statistics and news, potential customers for your business, and plans and successes of your competition. Regular study of these materials will also suggest to you which communications strategies might work for your own business.

Business-Oriented Media

If you live or conduct your business in a small town or rural area, your local newspaper may or may not have a business section, but it will have a business editor or reporter who is responsible for the business news. If your business is located in a large city, chances are there is at least one publication that specializes in reporting business news to the community, and probably more than one carries news and information of value to your business.

In addition, there are likely to be any number of specialized publications that report on narrower business topics within the city. Some may be daily newspapers, others may be weeklies, and still others may be business magazines or journals. In my own city, I've found some to be sold through subscriptions, while others are available free of charge because they are supported entirely by advertisers' revenues.

If you haven't done so already, identify these publications and begin reviewing several key ones on a regular basis. You especially need to identify those publications that are read by your target customers and provide information on your own industry, its market environment, and competitors.

Such publications sometimes carry advertisements from and news items about your competitors and their services, about pending legislation or regulations that might influence the viability of your business, and provide practical tips on doing business, as well as many other valuable informational items. For a comprehensive list of these publications for your area, ask your reference librarian to show you the *Editor and Publisher International Yearbook* (New York: Editor & Publisher Company) or the *Gale Directory of Publications and Broadcast Media.*

In most cases, the descriptions found in these directories will enable you to decide whether they are targeted toward your customers or cover your industry. If not, call them and request a review copy and a press kit. After all, you might wish to advertise in their newspaper or through their radio or television station. The press kits will contain statistics describing the media's readership or listening public and the types of programming emphasized.

PUBLIC RELATIONS VERSUS ADVERTISING

Owners of small businesses have to think about how to communicate with their intended customers. Advertising and public relations are two major communications options open to them and two major sources of market information for you. For some businesses in certain industries, display advertising in periodicals works well. By monitoring the press, marketing researchers will be able to track these advertisers through the ads they place. For other businesses, advertising in periodicals does not work well. More-over, advertising is expensive. If those businesses cannot create effective display advertising at a price they can afford, they have to look for alternatives. What can those businesses do?

They can seek free publicity, that's what. They can try to convince local editors to write articles about or profiles on them. They can try to appear on television or participate in talk shows. Each month, a press release can be sent to area newspapers, magazines, and radio and television stations announcing some newsworthy initiative—a new hiring, a promotion, plant openings or expansions, a speech given by the chief executive, or an employee being appointed to some government commission. This is common practice; I read somewhere that the *Wall Street Journal* gets 90 percent of its news from press releases.

Why do businesses send press releases? Because they work. They focus the public's attention on those businesses. They create name recognition. They attract attention to their causes. They place businesses in a good light and make them appear to be "good corporate citizens." They attract prospects to stores and businesses and help to enhance sales.

All of this effort by your competitors to attract publicity will make it easy for you to learn about them. When editors receive company press releases that interest them, they often follow up with a call to those companies, ask additional questions, and publish very revealing articles.

In my own area, for example, the local business press follows events in the health care arena very closely and reports weekly on financial information, market shares, key managers and employees, company problems, layoffs, hirings, and many other issues of interest to market researchers in competing companies. Not all of this information is sent to the media via press releases, of course. Reporters dig it out through company interviews, telephone queries, government reports and license applications, and court records. This researched business news represents a third source of market information for you.

If you develop a relationship with the reporters and editors who specialize in following your industry, you can sometimes learn important information about market events and competitors that never reaches the print or broadcast media. How might you develop such a relationship? By doing the same things your competitors are doing, of course. Send them your own press releases and follow up by telephone.

Once a relationship has been established, you can discuss many related issues, including articles that editors have written and facts missing from those articles, topics covered by their station or periodical, companies mentioned in past issues, and so forth. They will sometimes know exactly what you would like to know and would be only too happy to share their knowledge with you. In many cases, the editors or reporters will be able to help you find information not found elsewhere; they may know industry analysts, consultants, brokers, researchers, librarians, and experts all across the country and have their telephone numbers in their rolodex. Almost always, they will offer those names and numbers to you.

USING ADVERTISING INFORMATION FOR MARKETING RESEARCH

Newspapers, Radio, and Local Television

Advertisements provide an important source of market information to be found in your local newspapers, radio and television broadcasts, magazines, and even billboards. Among the questions that might be answered by looking at your competitors' ads are the following:

- Are your competitors expanding their work forces? (Check the want ads for open positions.)
- What sorts of employees are being sought by your competitors? (Read the qualifications and position descriptions in their help

wanted ads or call those competitors to request more information about their job listings.)

- What is the advertising strategy of your competitors? (Do they run institutional advertisements or promote sales of specific products? Do they rely on discount specials, appeals to luxury or image, or celebrity endorsements? How well is it working? (Once they initiate a strategy, do they continue it?)
- What are your competitors' advertising budgets for each periodical or medium? (If you note how frequently competitors advertise, you can estimate their advertising budget from the medias' rate cards.)
- What products are your competitors marketing? (What products are named in their advertisements?)
- What customers are being targeted by your competitors? (Men? Women? Families with children? Upscale? Downscale? What are the demographics and psychographics of the audience of the media used for advertising?)
- Which advertisements are working and why? (If advertisements are repeated several times, you can bet they are drawing customers. To find out why, call the medias' advertising managers—or the advertiser—and ask.)

If your business or market area is large enough to advertise in magazines, examine the advertisements in magazines or trade journals that target your demographic market. Mail-order businesses often place modest display ads in magazines to reach a large, well-targeted audience because magazines tend to be more narrowly focused in terms of readership or audience than newspapers or radio stations, with the notable exception of those papers and stations that serve specific ethnic, religious, or other groups.

Direct Mail

Direct mail is certainly not a part of the local press if you define the latter as newspapers, magazines, local radio, and the like, but direct mailings from your competitors can also provide a useful source of marketing research for you and your business.

Find out whether your competitors promote their products to your market through direct mail. If so, make sure that one of your family members or a relative does business with your competitors and asks to be placed on their mailing lists. Then, every time he or she receives a mailing from any of your competitors, add those mailers to your file on advertising. Study the types of mailings sent out as well as their frequency. Repeated mailings are one good indication that something is working.

Keep in mind, however, that not all direct mailings have the goal of generating immediate sales. Some may be intended only to convince the recipient to call. Others may simply be reminders that your competitor is the best source for items the recipient might want to buy later. And some might press for the recipient to make a purchase now.

Direct mail generally has a low response rate—sometimes as few as 1 percent of the mailers will produce a response. On the other hand, sometimes as many as 10 percent will generate a response, especially if the recipient is offered a gift or a premium for responding. Determine just what it is that the mailer is trying to convince the customer to do. Order a product? Come in to the store? Come by for a test drive? When you do receive a mailing from a competitor, assess it for its incentives for responses and the nature of the product being promoted.

Marketing research on these mailings can help you to understand the marketing strategies and tactics of your competitors and incorporate those that work into your own marketing plan.

THE TELEPHONE BOOK

Small business managers are very busy people. They don't have time to spend days in the library looking for and not finding materials about their markets, competitors, and products. To the greatest extent possible, they must have ready-at-hand sources of information at low cost and in convenient form.

Fortunately, one of the most valuable sources of market information has already been compiled for us: the telephone book. The telephone is truly the most taken-for-granted tool of modern business, and it is hard to imagine how modern business could be conducted without it.

With the telephone, we can reach virtually any other business in the world in a fraction of a second and at relatively low cost. Later in this book is a chapter on using the telephone to gather information, but in this chapter we focus on the telephone book. Virtually every household has access to a telephone book. Nearly all business offices are provided with an updated telephone book every year, because the telephone companies are constantly updating listings, correcting numbers and addresses, and adding new listings. Combine this resource with an inexpensive zip code directory and you have the basis for a mailing list of both residences and businesses in your market area.

Among the convenient features of this wonderful source of data are the following:

- The listings in telephone books are defined geographically and can be used to identify competitors and prospects within your market area.
- Business listings are generally set apart from residence listings, so if you are in a business that serves households or other businesses, you have a ready-made mailing list. (Business listings may omit office numbers, post office addresses, and zip codes in some cases, but you can get those by calling the establishment.)
- The yellow pages categorize businesses by product category.
- Yellow-page listings often tell a great deal about the size and products of the businesses.
- The sizes of ads within each category often tell much about the profitability of advertising in the yellow pages.

Defining the Market

For her marketing plan, each business manager must define the area that she believes comprises her market. A plumbing business may generate 90 percent of its business within 20 miles of its business location, but a mail-order business operated by a husband-and-wife team may market its product throughout the United States. Obviously, use of the telephone book as a marketing research tool may be more practical for the former than the latter.

One useful way to analyze the market's size would be to identify a competitor whose characteristics are similar to your own and then look in local telephone books to determine where those competitors are advertising. If you have no competitor, then identify a business similar in distribution methods, size, and character to your own and examine its advertising patterns.

Be aware that not all businesses will advertise in the yellow pages and that yellow-page advertising need not approximate the geographic scope of business operations. A marketing consultant, for example, may operate throughout the United States but keep a yellow-page listing only in his local yellow-page book. A mail-order business may do the same. On the other hand, each may advertise in specialized magazines, journals, or trade publications. So it is important to understand your own chosen industry and to understand the channels appropriate for making your business and telephone number accessible for that industry. Part of your research as an entrepreneur or business manager will be to identify those directories in which your own business should be listed so as to do you the most good in generating business.

For many small service businesses, however, the local yellow-page listings will provide an excellent information resource for market analysis. If you feel, for example, that you can realistically service customers within a 50-mile radius, then you can start by taking a map and compass and drawing a scaled circle around your business location representing that radius. The area within that circle is your primary market area. You may occasionally get business outside this circle but not very often. The primary market area usually accounts for 75 to 90 percent of your business.

Examine the cluster of cities and small towns in your primary market area and check your telephone book to see which of those towns are listed there. The towns and areas included in a telephone book are generally listed in its first several pages. If parts of your market area are not included in your local telephone book, call the number provided for customer service and ask in which books the missing towns and areas are included. You may then wish either to acquire those telephone books for business use or to consult with your local library for use of their copies.

For smaller market subdivisions (such as city blocks), consider contacting your State Library or telephone company to use a special edition of the telephone book that lists business and residential listings *in order of street address*. With this special edition, those homes or businesses located on a particular street will all be listed together.

Researching Your Competition

For those businesses listed under your business categories in the yellow pages, note any marketing information included in their listings. Large yellow-page ads often specify products, special services, areas of expertise, customer types sought, and skills offered. This information is placed into the ads by those hoping to differentiate themselves from their competitors and to attract inquiries from potential customers, but this information will also tell you where each competitor's market strengths might lie. If enough of your competitors in these listings specify their expertise, you can construct a fair representation of the major profitable market segments in your field.

Once you have identified your competitors, telephone them or, if possible, visit their business locations. Look around their facilities. If the expenditure is not great, buy something. Ask to be put on their mailing list. Ask about their services. Ask how large they are and how many employees are on the staff. If you decide that you would like to do business with them, ask what their policy might be about hiring you as a freelancer or subcontractor. Request marketing materials from each business. You may find that you can complement some of their services.

Analyze the relationship between the sizes of your competitors and the sizes of their yellow-page ads. Smaller businesses often have only a single line or two in the yellow pages, but not always. Large ads are expensive, so you are likely to find that larger firms are identified by their large ads. Directory sales staff will advise you to buy the largest ad you can afford, but doing so is not always wise. Research what your competitors are doing and find out why they made the choices they did.

Some firms purposefully de-emphasize certain of their services in yellow-page listings. For example, employment agencies provide job search assistance for job seekers for a fee, whereas Executive search consultants are paid by employers to locate executive or scarce technical talent. I know of an executive search firm that always buys a large, prominent ad under "Executive Search Consultants" in the yellow pages. It is also listed under "Employment Agencies" but buys only a one-line listing there.

Many businesses are listed under multiple headings because their product or service offerings overlap into a number of product categories. This practice, of course, can help you determine who might be a strong competitor and who might be weak. A business with its principal products or services in the same industry as your own is likely to be a serious competitor. But a large business with only a minor presence in your market may also be a major competitor. It will be difficult to determine who should be closely monitored unless you personally visit and study each firm. We'll discuss how to do this later.

Developing Prospect Mailing Lists

Any directory that lists the names, addresses, and telephone numbers of businesses and households is an obvious source of prospect mailing or calling lists. Although you could manually type these names and addresses into your database, there are more time-efficient ways to get the same or better information. These methods involve downloading mailing lists from CD-ROM at your local library or from on-line telephone directories and are discussed in later chapters.

THE LIBRARY AND OTHER SECONDARY SOURCES

5

Virtually all of us have used a library at one time or another. Libraries hold existing information, so when you are utilizing the library, you are essentially searching secondary data sources. Because secondary data was not prepared especially for your specific project, it may not precisely answer all your research needs. But in many cases, it can *almost* meet them. Moreover, in many instances secondary data is free of charge and can be retrieved far more swiftly than primary data. However, secondary information is not always free or inexpensive, so it will be worth your time to assess its value before spending more time and money to obtain it.

Remember trying to memorize the Dewey Decimal System in elementary school? Well, finding information is no easier today—if anything, it's more complex and confusing. There is no single, comprehensive resource for performing a full literature search. Some of the on-line databases are excellent, but even they have gaps. As well, information is stored and accessed today in a bewildering combination of print, microfiche, CD-ROMs, and electronic databases.

The purpose of this chapter is to help you find information either in your own library or in someone else's, but to find data today—and to access it—you may have to learn a few new skills not required even a couple of years ago. Readers in school during the late 1980s and early 1990s will be familiar with many of these skills. Older readers may need to seek out further instruction.

Therefore, this chapter will identify resources the reader can use to keep out-of-pocket outlays and time spent searching at a minimum. I will do that by identifying the places to look, the reference tools at hand to help you assess what is available at those "places," and the help—both human and electronic—you can call on to find and access your information as quickly as possible.

Technology has not only changed the way we identify sources of information but also revolutionized the way we access it. Just a few years ago, most information was inaccessible simply because it was stored somewhere other than where those who needed it happened to be. Today, distance is no barrier at all for the businessperson with just a few basic tools at hand.

THE REFERENCE LIBRARIAN

If you should happen to be a research pro, then you probably already know your way around your favorite library quite well. And you have developed a friendly and productive relationship with your reference librarian. But if it has been a while since you were in your library, then you might not know just what a reference librarian can do for you.

The reference librarian will know which major directories and reference sources are in the library and available for your use. Therefore, a telephone call to the reference librarian and a question about whether a particular directory is available might save you a half day if it is not (Figure 5.1).

FIGURE 5.1 The Reference Desk at the Library

My own local library system has a centralized reference desk telephone number that I can call to find out if this book or that magazine is at any of the county library sites. Find out if your own system has such a service. It will expand your reach into many area libraries before you commit time and energy to a fruitless trip to your local library.

The reference librarian, especially if she is employed by state or county government, will be especially cooperative in tracking down hard-to-find statistics, references, or facts for you. As a hard-pressed businessman, I appreciate the fact that I don't have to spend an unproductive day looking for an obscure piece of information when I have an expert supported by my tax money who can do it in 30 minutes.

Should you need to search the literature on a topic of importance to your business, call your local, state, and university libraries and ask for their policy about conducting literature searches for library patrons. Literature searches are usually expensive because they involve reviewing the on-line databases of commercial vendors. Some state libraries, however, will do searches for their citizens for free.

My state librarian recently told me a story about a patron who once used the West Virginia State Library. That library, he said, had a policy that every citizen of the state had the right to request at least one free on-line database search per month. This benefit is not trivial; each search can cost anywhere from $50 to $300. Fortunately, few West Virginians knew about this privilege, so he suspected that the library's search costs remained quite manageable.

THE LIBRARY CATALOG

First, let's get reacquainted with the catalog. In "the olde days," libraries had card catalogs containing hundreds of wooden drawers full of printed cards, and the only computers were mainframes that used punched paper cards. Today, technology has provided a more productive automated system for accessing information. The library catalog is now viewed through a personal computer network or terminal and stored on CD-ROMs.

But make no mistake—we are still in transition. For many years yet, you will probably have to consult both print and electronic reference resources to locate just the right information. No catalog or index now available is a comprehensive source of all the materials you might be looking for. Consequently, you will probably have to look in many places to find everything available on the topic you seek.

In any public library you are likely to find a computer-based catalog of the books, magazines, and other documents stored within the local library system. In my own state, the public libraries are operated by county government, so a number of libraries within each county are tied into one computer catalog system. Usually, library software permits searches for holdings by author, title, subject, and key words.

If you sit down at a terminal and do a search of all books and materials written on a particular subject, the system will most probably return a list of publications on that subject held by the county library system; tell you at which of the libraries those offerings are to be found; and tell you whether they are on the shelf, on reserve, or checked out.

If you go to another source, say the *Reader's Guide to Periodical Literature*, to search by that subject area, you will doubtless find many additional entries, none of which are housed at any of the libraries operated by your county. But you can probably gain access to those offerings, if you are patient, by asking the librarian to obtain those items for you through an interlibrary loan program.

However, printed indexes are very limited in the subject areas and key words by which materials were classified, and you could end up spending time searching under the wrong subject word. If you do a key word search, you will have little luck if you use a different key word than the one the publisher used in the index. How could you get around these problems? Your librarian knows that print and CD-ROM indexes use far fewer key words than online databases. Probably the best solution would be to request a literature search from your librarian.

THE BUSINESS REFERENCE DESK

Business users comprise one of the largest market segments of almost any public library, so you can be sure to find a business reference desk at most public libraries. Moreover, at many university libraries with a business collection, you may even find a business reference librarian.

THE *READER'S GUIDE* AND OTHER INDEXES

For searching through magazines, journals, newsletters, and other periodicals, you may have to seek out an appropriate readers' guide.[1] The *Reader's Guide to Periodical Literature* is probably the most well known of these. It is updated monthly and bound into annual volumes with indexes. However, the *Reader's Guide* covers fewer than two hundred magazines. Other sources identify far more magazines, journals, and books. There are, in fact, over one hundred special-purpose indexes in print covering far more sources than does the *Reader's Guide*. Ask your librarian for a copy of *Sheehy's Guide to Reference Books* for a directory of those indexes. If you are an entrepreneur considering entering the medicine industry, you really need to consult an index that will help you search through the medical literature rather than an all-purpose index such as the *Reader's Guide*.

Also, consult Lorna M. Daniell's *Business Information Sources* (Berkeley: University of California Press, 1993), for a listing and description of the extraordinary range of business information sources available. Also, see if your university library has its companion, *Business Reference Services*, by the same author. This is a reference list prepared for Harvard business students detailing sources of information about companies.

Although used primarily by journalists and freelance writers, *Writer's Market* (Cincinnati: Writer's Digest Books) lists more than four thousand consumer magazines and trade, technical, and professional journals as well as book publishers. *Writer's Market* is available at nearly all libraries or bookstores and is used by writers to research potential markets for their work. However, it is also very useful because it lists publications by subject area and by industry. When *Writer's Market* is updated each year, defunct publications are dropped from its listings, which is especially helpful in avoiding searching for and identifying out-of-print (and out-of-date) periodicals and information.

Use *Writer's Market* to find periodicals that may have information about your industry of interest. You will likely find many such publications in this manner that you won't find at any local library, so you may want to write to request sample copies. You may chose to subscribe to several to stay current on new developments in your industry. Consumer magazines are organized by subject; trade, technical, and professional journals are organized by industry.

Even more magazines and newspapers are listed in *Bacon's Publicity Checker* (*BPC*). *BPC* is a reference tool for public relations professionals to help them keep track of all the potential publications for promoting their clients. It is far more comprehensive than *Writer's Market* for identifying publications—perhaps too comprehensive for your needs. You may find it of value for your own public relations and advertising efforts, however.

Yet another reference source that is especially useful for locating newspapers is the *Gale Directory of Publications and Broadcast Media*. This reference lists over eleven thousand publishing companies with address, phone, and fax information as well as the publications they publish. It also lists and describes over thirty-eight thousand newspapers, magazines, journals, and other periodicals as well as radio, television, and cable stations and systems.

SELECTING REFERENCE LIBRARIES

You want to select a library that offers as comprehensive an offering of books, magazines, and reference materials as possible. Your state library or the library of a major university will probably provide the best service to you. After all, you will need quick and convenient access to information, and if your library does not store most of the resources you require for your marketing research, you will lose a great deal of time waiting for your needed materials to come in through the interlibrary loan program.

I use several wonderful libraries close at hand for my own research. I easily secured a library card from the library of my alma mater, the University of North Carolina. Some libraries allow businesses to apply for library cards for their employees. Other libraries have "friends of the library" programs; join and you qualify for a borrower's card. I was able to secure borrowing privileges from North Carolina State University by doing so.

However, more and more libraries are connecting into the Internet, and if you have a personal computer with a modem and an account with one of the increasing numbers of Internet on-ramp services, you will be able to communicate directly with these libraries.

SPECIAL LIBRARIES AND INFORMATION CENTERS

Often overlooked by the general public are thousands of special-purpose libraries and information centers. These libraries and special collections can be categorized as follows:

- Subject divisions, departmental collections, and professional libraries maintained by colleges and universities
- Branches, divisions, departments, and special collections in large public library systems that concentrate exclusively on one particular subject or group of subjects
- Company libraries that operate within the framework of a business or industry producing goods, services, or information for profit
- Governmental libraries, including those serving city departments, bureaus, and boards; state legislative reference libraries; libraries within federal departments, agencies, and military establishments; and divisions of national libraries
- Libraries supported by nonprofit organizations, associations, and institutions

Although the general public is not usually served by the librarians of these special libraries, occasionally professionals from public libraries and even market research professionals can secure the cooperation of library staff in identifying and securing specialized information. Should you fail to secure specific information elsewhere, you might try a telephone call to some of these libraries to see whether they can help. Alternatively, you might ask your public librarian to call for you.

To assess whether any of these special-purpose libraries might have the information you are looking for, refer to the *Directory of Special Libraries and Information Centers*, published by Gale Research of Detroit, Michigan, and very likely available at your local library. This directory lists almost twenty-two thousand special resource collections. The subject index of this directory classifies the libraries and information centers by the principle topics covered by their holdings.

An alternative to the Gale Research directory is the *World Guide to Special Libraries*, published by H.G. Saur of New York, which lists approximately thirty-two thousand libraries worldwide, including national libraries.

In the past, accessing information at these libraries was a nearly impossible task, but with the worldwide resource of the Internet, E-mail can be sent to many of these general and special libraries, requests can be made, and their data downloaded to your computer in a matter of hours or even minutes.

FEDERAL GOVERNMENT DATA

Some fourteen hundred libraries in the United States are government document depositories. These institutions receive government data and documents under the congressional library program of the Government Printing Office (GPO).

There are two categories of depository libraries: *regional* and *selective*. Regional depository libraries receive and retain one copy of every GPO publication—either in hard copy or microform—for use by the general public. Selective depository libraries receive only the publications chosen by their depository librarians as appropriate for their collections.

The basic collection of our depository libraries contains at least the following categories of GPO-printed materials:

Budget of the United States Government

Catalog of Federal Domestic Assistance

Census Bureau Catalog

Census of Housing (for state of depository only)

Census of Population (for state of depository only)

Code of Federal Regulations

Congressional Directory

Congressional District Data Book

Congressional Record

County-City Data Book

Federal Register

Historical Statistics of the United States

Monthly Catalog of United States Government Publications

Numerical Lists and Schedule of Volumes

Publications Reference File

Slip Laws (public)

Statistical Abstract

Statutes at Large

Subject Bibliographies (SB Series)

Supreme Court Reports

United States Code

United States Government Manual

Weekly Compilation of Presidential Documents

Check your library for the *Directory of U.S. Government Libraries* for a complete listing of all fourteen hundred libraries, their addresses, and their telephone numbers. Chances are you have at least a selective depository library close to you. More detailed descriptions of the individual depository collections may be found in the *Directory of Government Document Collections and Librarians.* All libraries in the United States (and its territories and possessions) that have one or more collections of documents are included in this directory, published by the Congressional Information Service, Inc., of Bethesda, Maryland.

To sift through this enormous volume of federal government–generated information, consider two sources for help. First, consult with the *federal documents librarian* at your chosen depository library. Knowledge of federal documents is a specialized field within the field of library science, and a talk with your federal documents librarian can save you a great deal of time.

Second, try consulting the reference library volume called *FedFind.* Published by ICUC Press, *FedFind* is designed to help the user get to the federal data he requires.

THE NATIONAL TECHNICAL INFORMATION SERVICE

Many new ventures during the 1990s are based on new technology or products. For today's entrepreneurs, monitoring technological developments and competitors using new technologies has become more important than ever.

In addition to trade journals, there are other sources of information for those seeking new product ideas, for example, the publications of the National Technical Information Service (NTIS).

NTIS is a government-created organization that supports its operations entirely through sales of its products and services. The NTIS database provides access to the results of U.S. government–sponsored research, development, and engineering plus analyses prepared by federal agencies, their contractors, and their grantees. Through NTIS, unclassified, publicly available, unlimited-distribution reports are made available for sale from agencies such as the National Aeronautics and Space Administration (NASA), the Department of Energy, the Department of Housing and Urban Development, the Department of Transportation, the Department of Commerce, and some six hundred other agencies. In addition, some state and local government agencies now contribute their reports to the database.

NTIS also provides access to the results of government-sponsored research and development from countries outside the United States. Organizations that currently contribute to the NTIS database include the Japan Ministry of International Trade and Industry (MITI), laboratories administered by the United Kingdom Department of Industry, the German Federal Ministry of Research and Technology (BMFT), the French National Center for Scientific Research (CNRSA), and many more.

NTIS makes available information on an astonishing range of technical subject areas, including

Administration and Management

Aeronautics and Aerodynamics

Agriculture and Food

Atmospheric Sciences

Behavior and Society

Biomedical Technology and Human Factors Engineering

Building Industry Technology

Business and Economics

Chemistry

Civil Engineering

Combustion, Engines, and Propellants

Communications

Computers, Control and Information Theory

Detection and Countermeasures

Electrotechnology

Energy

Environmental Pollution and Control

Government Inventions for Licensing

Health Planning and Health Services Research

Industrial and Mechanical Engineering

Library and Information Sciences

Manufacturing Technology

Materials Sciences

Mathematical Sciences

Medicine and Biology

Military Sciences

Missile Technology

NASA Earth Resources Survey Program

Natural Resources and Earth Sciences

Navigation, Guidance and Control

Nuclear Science and Technology

Ocean Technology and Engineering

Ordnance

Photography and Recording Devices

Physics

Problem-Solving Information for State and Local Governments

Space Technology

Transportation

Urban and Regional Technology and Development

Individuals may open accounts with NTIS by contacting its Office of Customer Services, 5285 Port Royal Road, Springfield, VA 22161. NTIS accepts most major credit cards.

STATE SOURCES OF INFORMATION

At the state level, several sources will be especially valuable to business users. First, consider contacting your State Data Center for assistance. Most states have one to serve as a state-level office for the U.S. Bureau of the Census.

At these centers, you will find people who will be very happy to help you look for your data and even conduct computer searches of census data for you. Usually, there is no charge for their service, and if there is a charge, it is generally *extremely* small.

The State Data Centers are an excellent source of consulting and research support for small businesses. They become, in effect, an extension of your own staff and are a wonderful resource. Consult with your state librarian for information on how to contact your own State Data Center or contact Tim Jones, State Data Center Office, U.S. Department of Commerce, Bureau of the Census, Washington, D.C. 20233-0001; (202) 457-1305.

Another marvelous source of support for the entrepreneur or small business owner are the State Libraries, which are the depositories and archives for each state's records. As in the State Data Centers, staff members are supported by state tax revenue and are therefore expected to be responsive to information requests from the public. Ofttimes, staffing is limited, so the help that staff members offer may be minimal. But at many of these libraries, the public does not realize what resources are available, so demand on librarians' time is not overwhelming. If you ask for consultative help, literature searches, and even database searches, you may find that they are only too glad to help at no cost to you.

OTHER STATE AND LOCAL SOURCES

Want to secure a map of your market area? Try your state's Department of Transportation or your county's land and titles office for specialized area maps. In your county's property titles office, you will find a surprising amount of available information about your competitors' property holdings and their owners. Of course, you will find records about your own property there, too.

ELECTRONIC RESOURCES

Books in Print

Bookstores and most libraries will have a reference volume called *Books in Print* published annually by R. R. Bowker Company of New York. Generally, *Books in Print* will list those books that are, strangely enough, still being printed. Most libraries will have *Books in Print* stored on a CD-ROM from the same publisher, and by using the library's CD-ROM reader, you will be able to recall listings by author, title, or subject.

Should you be searching the literature for older documents or books, Bowker Electronic Publishing Company also markets a companion CD-ROM called *Books Out of Print*. Many libraries will have this electronic publication as well.

CD-ROM Documents

As CD-ROM readers have been added to the computer systems at libraries, the assortment of publications available on CDs has skyrocketed (Figure 5.2). In the past, most of the data stored on these CDs could only be browsed, but increasingly the disks and library

FIGURE 5.2   Using Computers (top) and CD-ROM Readers
(bottom) at the Library

equipment permit users to download their desired information to their own floppy disk and take it home or to the office.

At my own state library, the following CD-ROM titles were available:

The American Business Disk

Books in Print

Books Out of Print

Business Periodicals Index

CCH-Access

Census of Agriculture

Census of Population and Housing

Compton's Multimedia Encyclopedia

County Business Patterns

Directory of Library and Information Professionals

Dun's Business Locator

Dun's Middle Market Disc

Dun's Million Dollar Disc

Economic Censuses

Encyclopedia of Associations

Government Printing Office (GPO) Monthly Catalog

Grolier New Multimedia Encyclopedia

Library Literature

Library Reference Plus

Literary Index

Magazine Article Summaries

Moody's Company Data

National Economic, Social & Environmental Databank

National Trade Databank

Public Affairs Information Service (PAIS)

PC-SIG

Regional Economic Information System (REIS)

Small Business Consultant

Statistical Abstract of the United States

Thomas Register

Ulrich's Plus

U.S. Exports of Merchandise

U.S. Imports of Merchandise

If you are putting together a business plan, go to these disks first. In an hour, you might have all the market data you'll ever need or want.

On-line Databases

In addition to CD-ROM databases, users also have access to enormous on-line databases. Some of these can be accessed through the major on-line services, such as CompuServe, America Online, or Delphi. Users of the Internet can also directly access the same databases if they establish an account with those vendors.

For a comprehensive list of on-line databases and descriptions of the various types of data on each, consult the *Gale Directory of Databases* published by Gale Research of Detroit, Michigan. The most recent of these directories contains information on over nine thousand on-line databases, three thousand producers, eight hundred on-line services, and nine hundred vendors of database products. Recent consolidations have added coverage of CD-ROM, diskette, magnetic tape, handheld, and batch-access database products to this directory.

USING THE TELEPHONE

6

Marketing researchers use the telephone to

- Conduct exploratory interviews and structured surveys to gather primary data (Figure 6.1)
- Access on-line services, news groups, bulletin boards, and E-mail
- Access other secondary sources of data such as libraries and on-line databases

Businesspeople doing their own marketing research should not assume that all marketing research involves complicated surveys. In fact, much research is of a very informal or *ad hoc* character. Quite a lot of useful information can be gathered through casual exploratory conversations with customers, prospects, suppliers, researchers, and media representatives. To save a lot of time traveling and arranging interviews, however, consider using the telephone instead.

FIGURE 6.1   The Telephone Is an Essential Tool for Marketing Research

VOICE SURVEYS

Exploratory and Experience Interviews

Much research is accomplished using exploratory research methods. For example, consider a computer retailer selling small systems and software. She might wish to know which brands other retailers were marketing in her immediate area and decide to check their prices so as to compare them to her own prices. She would probably first look in the yellow pages for the telephone numbers of other retailers in the area and then call each of them, ask for a

74

salesperson, and explain that she needed to gather some pricing information on available systems.

If her information needs were somewhat more complex—if, for example, she wanted to do some strategic planning about which brands and capabilities she should carry in the future—she might try an experience survey. If the market were to shift away from systems based on the 8086 architecture to, say, the Power PC chip, she would want to begin establishing a support capability for the new architecture by training sales staff, bringing Power PC prototypes into her product line, and locating repair staff with the right technical background.

To find out what the experts think about the Power PC chip's prospects, she might try an experience survey of industry experts. First, she might do a literature search of articles in the prominent computer magazines by accessing the Ziff Net articles databases through CompuServe. She would look for information published within the last year on the Power PC chip, its capabilities, and its prospects. Then she might try to call some of the authors of particularly insightful articles about the chip's prospects. Next, she might call on her industry association to request the names of people who might be able to add to what she had learned from the published articles and their authors.

Open-ended questions leave the nature of responses open to the person being interviewed. In open-ended interviews, ask for the facts supporting expert viewpoints, question any inconsistency among experts, and ask about supporting documentation in the written materials you've examined. In these types of surveys, there is a certain element of risk that the information will not be accurate. Not only do you not generally have any way of determining the expertise level of each respondent, but also you are not interviewing a representative sample of people. And remember, you are asking these experts to predict the future, so you will need to use your informed judgment to decide whether or not to accept their opinions.

Structured Telephone Interviews

If you feel that you need to do a structured set of telephone interviews, consider preparing a questionnaire. Later, in chapter 11 we will discuss

- How to draw a random sample
- How to put together a survey form
- How to order your questions in a questionnaire
- What kinds of questions to ask
- How to measure responses
- How to summarize your survey data for analysis

In this chapter, however, we consider only how to use the telephone as an information-gathering instrument.

The telephone is an *intrusive* data collection instrument. Your call interrupts people during their daily work schedule or leisure time. You yourself have probably been called to the telephone in the late evening or on weekends by someone who launches into a sales presentation. If your experience with these telemarketers has been like mine, you usually tell them you are not interested, but the salesperson refuses to hang up and continues to try to close a sale. In a survey, you are not trying to close a sale. In gaining a respondent's cooperation, your only resource is your nonthreatening persuasion and the respondent's own curiosity.

When you are conducting an interview, remember that you are asking a person to do something for you for no compensation. Moreover, you are probably going to ask them at least one question that the respondent will consider intrusive, personal, or simply none of your business. So how will you get them to cooperate with you in spite of all this? There are several rules that should help.

1. Be friendly, unaggressive, but persistent. Respondents will either willingly give you the information you wish or resist. If they resist and you insist, you may find them giving purposefully inaccurate information out of irritation with you or hang-

ing up on you before the interview has been completed. Remember, people like to be asked for their opinions. And my experience has been that many people enjoy participating in a real survey.

2. Tell them why their ideas and opinions are important. The information may be important only to you, but that's not necessarily a poor reason. After all, you are taking the time to call people and ask for their opinions. Don't rush them through an interview. Give them the courtesy of your time and your complete attention while on the phone. And tell them what difference their opinions might make in your business.

3. Tell them right up front that you will not try to sell them anything and that you only want to ask for their opinions about your research subject. This is so important that I try to make this point my first comment after I introduce myself when I am doing a survey.

4. Assure them that you will hold their answers in confidence and that their names and answers will not be given to anyone. This assurance is not necessarily important in surveys that do not touch on sensitive or controversial subjects, but the respondent doesn't know that before you administer the survey. So make it clear from the start.

5. Use screening questions to make sure that you are speaking with the correct person for your survey.

6. Keep your interview fairly short—no more than five minutes if possible. If the interview is likely to be longer than that, tell them it will likely take 10 or 15 minutes and offer to call back at a more convenient time. The longer surveys are more likely to be rescheduled to a later date by your respondents.

7. Avoid speaking in a monotone. Animate your voice and sound enthusiastic. You stand a better chance of raising the curiosity of your respondents if you sound interesting.

To make sure that all these rules are followed, try writing a script to persuade your respondents to agree to an interview. With a script, you will not forget to mention any of these points or to screen your respondents. A model script is displayed in Figure 6.2 for you to modify for your own questionnaires. Make your own script as informal as possible and try to create a relationship with each person you call. A business-to-business survey would be conducted in a very similar way, so this script—which is a bit lengthy—could be used for either a consumer interview or a business interview.

ACCESSING INFORMATION ELECTRONICALLY

Daniel Burrus, in his book *Technotrends* (New York: HarperCollins, 1994), argues that the U.S. economy is exiting the Information Age and entering the Communications Age. By this, he means that we are developing the technology to access the information we want when we need it but not be barraged by information we don't require.

Making Use of the Services of Your Telephone Company

Both the local operating companies and the long-distance carriers offer a variety of services to businesses. If you call your local telephone company and ask for their small business services consultant, you can obtain a list and description of the services available to you as a small business owner or manager. Although these services are designed for everyday business, creative application of these technologies to information gathering will enable you to get to critical information in the minimum time and at a very reasonable cost.

Most of the regional telephone companies are now making available electronic white pages that can be accessed by personal

CONSUMER SURVEY

Opening Telephone Script

Hello. My name is Roger Smith of AtHome Computer Services. I am calling homes in the Baltimore area to do a survey on how computers are being used in the home. I am not selling anything and will not discuss any products for sale. No salesperson will call after we speak.

I was given your number by the XYZ company because your family purchased a home computer from XYZ last year, and XYZ thought someone in your family might be able to give me some informed opinions.

I need to speak with someone who knows how your computer is used. Would that be you? (*If not, ask who would be the most appropriate person to speak with. When that person comes to the telephone, ask: "Is this* _____ *?"*)

Repeat your greeting and explanation if necessary and continue below.

I'd like very much to spend about five minutes on the telephone to get your thoughts about how your family uses the computer in your home. Your thoughts are important because I want to use survey results to decide what kinds of support my store should provide to computer owners like yourself. I can use your opinions to decide what spare parts to keep in inventory, what training to provide my staff, and how best to support home computer user service needs. I promise to keep your opinions confidential and will not release your name to anyone else for any reason.

Can we talk now, or would a later time be more convenient? *If you have to reschedule, what time?* _____
what date? _____

FIGURE 6.2   Telephone Survey Introduction Script

computer via modem. You can obtain up-to-the-minute listings of the names, addresses, and telephone numbers of individuals and companies throughout your own state and in other states from the FCC data stream.

Accessing this service from your office or home personal computer, you can conduct key name searches throughout your local areas. Suppose you wish to find out about a competitor's store locations. You can do a search of a range of area codes, and the database will be scanned to find all matches.

A number of service bureaus throughout the United States are making these databases available to the public, including AT&T. As yet, there are few electronic yellow pages because the telephone companies are not convinced that such a product would be profitable. You should contact your local telephone company for help in identifying the closest supplier.

You can also identify competitors or customers operating within an area by using the telephone company's find-it service. If you sold plumbing supplies, for example, you would dial the telephone number of the telephone company's locator service and obtain a list of plumbers operating in your market of interest, including their locations and their telephone numbers. This information would be more recent than your local yellow pages because newly listed plumbers would also be included and out-of-business plumbers would be absent.

Purchasing a voice mailbox with the local telephone company could also save you a great deal of time. Interested persons could use it to respond to your advertisements or surveys, and their responses would be left for you to review at a convenient time.

In some instances, your telephone company can give you the telephone number of persons calling you. These numbers and the identity of the callers can be important information to be added to your records on customers, prospects, and competitors in your marketing databases.

The capability to arrange for teleconferencing permits you to set up informal audio focus groups for research purposes. Although some disadvantages can result from not having your participants face to face, your participant fees can be lower because conferences can be shorter and more convenient for participants. In the near future, telephones with video screens will enable such groups to see and react to one another. Moreover, you don't have to provide refreshments or reimburse participants for travel expenses.

There are, of course, many other services that may be useful in identifying information sources and gathering data for the creative researcher. Among these services are

- Your telephone usage statements (which contain some very useful marketing data if you chose to utilize it)
- 800 and 900 numbers
- Your long-distance bill
- New telephone company services

One potentially valuable service being considered by some telephone companies is a fax number directory. But by using your own carefully developed list of customer and prospect fax numbers, you can implement a survey in quick order and with extremely low expenditures. With such a directory, surveys could be faxed overnight by your computer to a sample of customers or potential customers. Conceivably, you could have your answers faxed back to you before close of business on the next day.

Even small businesses that lack a fax machine or PC with a fax card can take advantage of this technology by calling on their long distance carrier. For example, Sprint provides a fax service called Broadcast Distribution. With this service, a businessperson can mail or modem a survey form directly to Sprint, and Sprint will broadcast it by fax to a list of numbers you provide. Survey respondents can then fax their answers back or call their responses in to your voice mailbox or 800 number.

Marketing Research with 800 and 900 Numbers

With new FCC regulations, access to 800 numbers is within the reach of all businesses for a very modest monthly cost in addition to long-distance charges. 800 numbers are typically free to the caller because user charges are paid by the recipient.

Given a choice, most people would rather call than write, and you can take advantage of this preference by allowing them to call in information to you free of charge rather than writing their responses. Using 800 numbers, your response rate may well be higher than it would have been if you had used a mail survey. Moreover, should you have a large number of simple responses coming in by telephone, you might try routing them to your electronic mailbox maintained by the telephone company or to your own staff of survey people. Of course, the recording that greets your respondents should be appropriate to encourage them to provide their answers. A promise of an incentive gift or premium for their help might pay dividends.

The use of 900 numbers in marketing research is a idea that has yet to be widely tried. However, national television programs have been experimenting with this approach by urging viewers to call one of two 900 numbers to vote yes or no on some question or issue. Typically, only persons who are seriously involved in the issue respond. Costs for these calls may be as high as $3.00 a minute, and the *caller* pays for the calls.

Using 900 numbers as an income-generating device is currently a popular entrepreneurial activity throughout the United States, but it has been dominated by large service bureaus because of the capital investment required. Among the most popular ideas have been introduction or dating services, psychic advisors, and information services. If your product or service complements or supplements these types of services, they can be useful as sources of surveying and calling lists.

Take Advantage of Telephone Company Reporting Capabilities

Telecommunications services are increasingly being packaged in more economical groups, and with this packaging comes greater opportunities for management reports, which enable small businesses to track their operating and research costs better. Sprint, for example, promotes a package of reporting software called FON-VIEW@ that permits the calculation of cost per interview, enables you to graph trends in research costs, and creates research reports.

Simply spending time analyzing your small business's telephone bill can pay big dividends in understanding your markets. For example, suppose you have your customers use a certain set of telephone lines. Prospects, on the other hand, are supplied with different numbers to call. From these invoices, you can find out who calls your office most often. Where are they calling from? Why are they calling? Create a profile of your incoming calls to understand your customers' needs better and to compare them with those of prospects.

Marketing Research on the Internet

Everywhere one goes these days, the Internet is being discussed. The Internet is essentially a large number of computers that are linked together through the telephone lines. These computers are called *servers*. Servers are simply computer storage depots for programs, files, and data.

As with discussions about any computer-based tools, discussions of the Internet are dominated by technical terminology. As software is developed to simplify the task of using the Internet, the technical terminology will drop by the wayside for the everyday user, but for now, you had better prepare to spend some time learning new words and concepts.

Buy yourself a good how-to book on using the Internet and spend a few cold winter evenings curled up with it. There are many good books available. I will name only two for the sake of brevity:

- Ed Krol, *The Whole Internet: Users Guide and Catalog* O'Reilly & Associates, Inc., 103 Morris Street, Suite A, Sebastopol, CA 95472; telephone (800) 998-9938.
- John Levine, *Internet for Dummies* (San Mateo: IGG Books, 1994). This guide can be downloaded from many sources on the Internet, but it can also be purchased from your neighborhood bookstore as well.

To access information anywhere on the Internet, you require a *gateway*. To provide this service to researchers, hobbyists, and businesses, a group of service companies have sprung up to provide on-ramps to the Internet for you and me. For a monthly fee, an on-ramp service will provide you with the following:

- A national mailbox address for receiving electronic mail from anywhere in the world
- The ability to upload or download files from other servers/ locations on the Internet
- Access to discussion groups on subjects that (hopefully) will be relevant to your business interests
- Access to library catalogs and government documents throughout the entire world, and more

Unfortunately, you can also waste a vast amount of time knocking around the Internet with few results if you are not careful. The amount of information available is huge beyond imagination, but because the network is still very new, the tools for navigating it are still being developed. If you are just getting started with the Internet, you are likely to find it confusing and incredibly disorganized. In short, it will take you some time to learn how to use this resource economically.

Several user tools (software) are available or are being developed to make the Internet easier to navigate and use. This software can be added to your own personal computer to give you a user-friendly interface to the Internet. Some of this software is available from commercial software outlets, and some is available free of charge from your Internet service bureau once you have set up an account.

There are other search tools located on your service bureau's server to help you find information of particular interest. Some of those are summarized in the following list:

- Gopher—A software application that presents you with a series of predesigned menus for accessing information from collaborating Gopher server sites on the Internet. If your information category is identified in a menu, then you will be automatically connected to the information's location—even if that location is in Germany, Australia, Brazil, or San Francisco. There are many university libraries linked into the Gopher net.
- Telnet—A network of government and university computers bound together by an agreement to provide their services on-line to the public and university communities. You don't really require an Internet service bureau to access Telnet and the resources of its member institutions. You can probably access this network by dialing up your area university's on-line library catalog. Telnet utilizes your personal computer as a terminal and is reasonably simple to use. The user is presented with sets of menus through which he or she can navigate to get to the information desired.

  Of special value to the market researcher will be the databases of journal, newspaper, and business periodical articles accessible through Telnet.
- Wide Area Information Servers (WAIS)—WAIS allows you to search through the Internet for articles containing combinations of key words. It is based upon the development of article indexes on many specialized subjects and references to the articles and materials (wherever they may be housed) described by the indexes.

However, WAIS works only for those articles that have been indexed. If articles that might be important to you have not been indexed, then WAIS won't find them. And it works for those articles only if you guess the correct combination of key words by which the desired articles have been indexed. WAIS searches these indexes—not the original articles themselves— and there are many indexes. Some of them are good and others are poor. On a given topic of interest to you, there may be no good index in existence. Your service bureau may be able to help you determine whether an index exists, and if so, how to access it.

- The World-Wide Web (WWW)—The World-Wide Web (often referred to as the Web) is the newest technology to emerge to assist you in finding information of interest. Developed by the European Particle Physics Laboratory, it is being used by people throughout the world to find information on virtually any subject. It is based on the concept of *hypertext* searches.

To try the Web, you might acquire and install a Web browser software package on your own personal computer or access the package through Telnet. Currently, one of the most popular of the Web interfaces is a program called Mosaic. Once you are enrolled with a local Internet service bureau, this program will probably be available for downloading from your service to your personal computer, and you can then install it on your hard disk. The net browser called Netscape has recently by-passed Mosaic in popularity.

An excellent source of ideas, feedback, and good (and bad) judgment about common problems is the Internet's selection of discussion or "news" groups (Usenet). You can find a server that hosts discussions on every imaginable subject, and in that selection, you will doubtless be able to find several that are useful to you in gathering marketing information for your small business. Many consultants haunt the byways of these discussion groups seeking opportunities for new business, leads, and ideas for new ventures. You can do the same.

Take Advantage of the Major On-line Services

For a modest monthly fee plus on-line charges, you can log onto any of several general on-line information services at any time. Most are open 24 hours a day. Nearly everyone is now familiar with at least the names of some of these services: CompuServe, Prodigy, America Online, GEnie, Delphi, eWorld, and DataTimes are the names of several currently available.

These information services provide E-mail addresses, file upload and download services, and access to numerous databases. They also provide discussion forums and access to the Internet. CompuServe is currently the largest, with about 2.3 million members and many services for the business user. America Online is second, with 1.1 million members, but it is growing much faster than CompuServe. Prodigy is third in size and is designed mostly for the home user.

Although the costs of doing your own on-line searches of databases can be significant, by using services such as CompuServe or America Online you can conduct your searches quickly without leaving your house or business and make your searches during those times when you are less pressed, such as evenings and weekends.

The cost of database searches on such services as CompuServe, moreover, are quite reasonable. Here is a sample of some of the databases easily accessible to you through CompuServe:

Supersite Demographics Database—Available to Executive Service members, the Supersite Database provides demographic and sales potential reports for the entire United States or any state, county, zip code, metropolitan area, place, census tract, or other market-defined geographic area (Nielsen TV Market, Arbitron TV Markets). Reports cover general demographics, income, housing, education, employment, and current and projected year forecasts.

Demographic Reports—Provides detailed demographic reports based on the 1990 Census and covering population, housing, ethnicity, age, and income. Reports range in price from $25 to $45 apiece.

Knowledge Index Database—Provides access to over one hundred separate databases on business practices and trends, full-text articles, newspaper articles and features, books in print and out of print, business press releases on Businesswire Service, U.S. and Canadian business coverage, international trade, dissertation abstracts, economic literature indexes, technical journals and encyclopedia, legal resource indexes, and so forth. Even the *Washington Post Online* is found here.

State and County Demographics Databases—Provides access to several large databases including the Business Demographics Database, the Census Database, the Neighborhood Reports Database, U.S./State/County Reports, Information USA, the National Technical Information Service (NTIS) Database, and a database of U.S. government publications from the Government Printing Office.

The U.S./State/County Reports—Provide demographics for the entire United States, any state, or any county. Cost: $10 per report.

Business Database Plus—Provides access to the Integrated Business and Trade Information Database for access to five years of full-text articles from more than seven hundred and fifty business magazines, trade journals, and regional business newspapers. Also provides access to two years of articles from a variety of specialized business newsletters. Business Demographics Database users pay $0.25 per minute in connect charges plus $1.50 for any portion of an article that is viewed or downloaded.

Neighborhood Demographics Database—Provides demographic reports for individual zip codes. Cost per report: $10.

Thomas Register—Provides in-depth information on individual companies with descriptions of the products they produce and market. Individual searches cost $7.50 in addition to connect charges and base connect rates.

The Marketing/Management Research Center—Provides quick access to many databases containing full text of major U.S. and international business, management, and technical literature; market and industry research reports; marketing studies and statistical reports; U.S. international company press releases; and practical how-to guides for owning and operating a small business. Costs are quite reasonable, ranging from $2 per search to $15 per report.

The National Technical Information Service—Provides information on research sponsored by the U.S. and other national governments. Cost of searches retrieving up to ten titles: $3. Additional searches cost $3 for each group of ten titles retrieved.

During 1995, MCI Telecommunications is expected to create its own on-line service called internetMCI, and Microsoft Corporation will create yet another to be called Microsoft Network.[1]

Although these general information services are not specifically focused toward commercial transactions, several more specialized ventures are. The Enterprise Integration Network (EINNet), for example, is a joint venture of Sprint and the Microelectronics and Computer Technology Corporation (MCC). This consortium provides an on-line service focusing on commercial transactions. Member companies can advertise in a yellow pages–like directory of goods and services as well as prospect and take orders among other members for business.

Other on-line services include the following:

- Entrepreneurs Online—An on-line service for entrepreneurs providing round tables for conversation, E-mail, business leads, advertising opportunities, capital sources databases, and references to consultants to work with start-up businesses; telephone number (800) 784-8822.

89

- International Trade Network—An on-line service for scouting for trade leads abroad, researching import-export services and overseas investments, and advertising. Send E-mail to mayordomo @world.std.com.
- Entrepreneurial Edge Online—An on-line service providing tutorials for entrepreneurs; telephone (800) 220-9553.[2]

Other specialized commercial services include Mead Data Central, Dow/Jones News/Retrieval, and Dialog Information Services.

Other Electronic Devices for Retrieving Information

As entrepreneurs (or prospective entrepreneurs), we all need a network of advisors, colleagues, and fellow students of the marketplace. Mostly, these are people we work with or see daily, but there is really no need to restrict ourselves to local people when we have a window to the world through our personal computers.

Just as we might select a favorite assortment of publications to review regularly for important information on our markets, competitors, and products, there are likely to be bulletin boards or discussion (news) groups we might monitor electronically. Suppose, for example, that you are a marketing consultant working in Boston and you find through your professional association that a bulletin board for marketing professionals is being operated by a firm in Dallas. You could check directly into that bulletin board, say on a weekly basis, by paying long-distance rates and then use E-mail to post questions, request information, and even register advertisements for your own services. Pretty soon, you would have a national network of people with similar interests and problems with whom to discuss your information needs. Many of those persons might have exactly the information you need or know where to find it.

Alternatively, you might ask your local bulletin board operators to determine whether any of them are members of *FidoNet*—a network of bulletin boards that cooperate in transferring files among themselves. Currently, there are more than twenty-five thousand bulletin boards in the FidoNet network, so it is likely that one is nearby your home or office.

The advantage of using the services of this network is, of course, that you use local telephone service and often don't have to pay long-distance rates to route your messages to the destination bulletin board. You can very easily set up a survey to be electronically distributed to all the other FidoNet bulletin boards. Respondents could send their answers back to you at your "home" bulletin board or address responses to your Internet address.

Boardwatch magazine estimates that there are at least sixty thousand public bulletin board systems (BBSs) operating today in the United States. Chances are that many of these are utilized by people just like your customers, prospects, or suppliers. By checking in occasionally on those BBSs, you can leave questions, survey documents, or requests for ideas on problems you all share that will bring you a deluge of electronic mail. You can then download that mail and peruse it at your leisure.

You may find it of value to create your own BBS to provide information, files, or service for your own customers, prospects, or suppliers. It would be a simple step to set up your own survey to be presented to everyone who checks into your bulletin board.

Another source of specialized business information are the electronic clipping services. You can subscribe to these services and have them regularly place new clippings in your electronic mailbox on subjects you specify. These services are especially useful for gathering current information on competitors. The numbers of these clipping services are constantly growing, but these are two of the most well known:

- Bacon's Clipping Bureau, Chicago, Illinois
- Burrell's Press Clipping Service, Livingston, New Jersey

REAL INTELLIGENCE TRICKS OF THE TRADE

7

Although originally a subfield of marketing research, *competitive intelligence* has evolved into a discipline of its own. It can be defined narrowly or broadly, depending upon your philosophy. In its narrowest definition, it refers to the collection and interpretation of information about a single competitor. In its broader definition, it can encompass information about not only one firm but also an entire industry and the environment. However you define it, a major focus in conducting competitive intelligence is on firms that have the same or similar customers and suppliers as your own.

The scale of a firm's competitive intelligence activities will depend upon how it defines its business. For example, if you were the manager of a local movie theater, you might wish to consider competition from video rental stores in case the film you are considering rebooking is available at a local department store for a $1 rental fee. You might also wish to consider checking on the programming of local television stations in the event your major feature is showing at the same time as the Superbowl. In considering these alternative sources of entertainment, you are acknowledging the fact that you are in the entertainment business rather than simply the movie business. If that is the case, you have a much larger number of potential competitors to track.

WHY GATHER COMPETITIVE INTELLIGENCE?

To Anticipate Change

As technological advances have assumed greater importance in lowering product costs, expanding product capabilities, and enhancing organizational flexibility, it has become more important to know what technologies your competition is using. And as international competition has crept into even small towns and rural areas, it has become more important than ever to consider what companies thousands of miles away are planning or not planning.

During the 1960s and 1970s, the U.S. electronics industry found out to its dismay that Japanese manufacturers could manufacture and distribute higher-quality electronic consumer goods in the United States at a lower price than it could. Today, researching trends in your industry has become just good business policy.

To Make Strategic Decisions

Even single entrepreneurs operating small service businesses had better know what their competitors are doing and how they are doing it, or else their survival may be threatened. If you are a local consultant, are consultants from multinational firms calling on your clients? How do you stack up against their expertise and resources? Can you compete directly, or should you shift to a niche that they don't threaten? Researching your competition can help identify how your business can survive in the face of a constantly changing market.

DEFINING STRATEGIC INFORMATION NEEDS

Businesses concern themselves with competitive intelligence to

- Devise defensive strategies to protect their market position and client base
- Gain a long-term advantage over competitors

Thus, competitive intelligence is concerned first and foremost with identifying and locating *strategically important* information and only secondly with *tactical* information. Strategic advantage tends to provide a long-term gain against competitors and affects such factors as production costs, distribution channel control, gaining a strategic position in the market, becoming more customer oriented, and gaining control of the pace of new product development.

Historically, the word *strategy* applied to military campaigns and dealt with the moves and countermoves of combatants. Knowing the plans of your foe can obviously create an advantage for your side when your survival is on the line. The application of military terms and strategies to business tactics has not been without its critics, however. Historians recall for us the methods of the infamous "Robber Barons" of the late 1800s and early 1900s as a warning about predatory business practices, but still the concept endures.

Today, practitioners of competitive intelligence do have their code of ethics, but outside the profession, amateur sleuths are not bound by any such code.

Those who pursue strategic advantages over competitors view competitive intelligence as key information. They view the world in terms of strategic positioning, long-term strengths and weaknesses, and moves and countermoves, and they focus on six different kinds of information:

- Competitors
- Products
- Marketplace

- Technology
- Environment
- Customers and prospects

You may think that small companies and entrepreneurs don't need to worry about strategic planning and research. Those are things the big boys do, not the little guys. Well, that may be true about the big competitors, but that doesn't mean strategic thinking is not meaningful for entrepreneurs or small businesses. Coming to understand your competition through research can mean the difference between survival and failure in business.

Ask the convenience stores and small boutiques who went out of business when the Sam's Clubs or Wal-Marts moved in whether they should have worried about the moves of large competitors. The "little guy" has never been more vulnerable to threats by larger firms and even international competition than today.

Small farmers follow the weather in other countries to determine what competition might flow from bumper crops in Mexico, Canada, or Europe. In the software business, small firms are being swallowed up by giants because they lack the resources to combat the giants. Even the small businessperson must ask herself if her business is strategically vulnerable to competitors.

It is not necessary for the small business manager or entrepreneur to go through the elaborate strategic planning process followed by large corporations to think strategically. The essence of strategic thinking may not be in planning at all but in reacting quickly to strategic threats to avoid direct competition from overwhelming market power.

One way to avoid competition is to select *innovation strategies* in product development. Avoid bringing products to market that closely duplicate those of major competitors. Small software companies, for example, can thrive by creating applications that complement the products of major players, thus turning their competitive relationship into a strategic partnership. Small businesses and entrepreneurs are the guerilla fighters of the marketplace. They frequently prosper by finding the gaps in the market, by serving the underserved, by innovating rather than competing directly, and by providing superior service to a narrowly defined niche in the market that is too small to be of interest to bigger players. How do they know where those gaps are? They research their competitors.

Simply moving your store location or concentrating upon potential customers at a distance from major metropolitan areas may be a smart strategic response to a large competitor moving into your local market. But if you are not monitoring the competition, you may be caught with a newly signed lease on your building and no way to move.

Small concerns take advantage of the fact that larger competitors are more concerned with sales than service after the sale. Or they might offer service on products not carried by larger competitors. Whatever the strategy may be, the small business can react to superior market power intelligently only by understanding the strengths and weaknesses of the competition.

There are many opportunities waiting for businesspeople who know the gaps in the market's product and service mix. Alternatively, failure of the smaller businessperson to know and anticipate the moves of his competition can easily lead to his downfall.

DEVELOPING PROFILES OF YOUR COMPETITORS

Determining What Data You Should Collect

Even the largest corporation cannot afford gathering endless amounts of information on its competitors. The gathering process must be guided by some kind of prioritizing process that determines the kinds of information that are most important for the firm.

One approach to prioritizing information requirements is to identify the *strategic keys* for your business, which are those things your business must do well to be successful. Strategic keys can be classified under the following categories:

- Characteristics of the firm
- Industry characteristics
- Business characteristics
- Environmental factors

Characteristics of the firm are those strategic keys that relate to the success of a specific business enterprise but not necessarily of other firms within the industry. If your firm specializes in marketing extraordinarily good security systems for small businesses, then the quality and cost of the technology underlying your systems is a strategic key for your firm. If you run a consulting firm, then the quality of your consultants is critically important to the success of your business.

Industry characteristics are strategic keys associated with the products or firms in an industry or the way business is conducted in a particular industry. For example, if you were in the agricultural feeds business, the ability to make deliveries to customers' farms or barns might be a strategic key.

Business strategic keys relate to the things that must be done to operate a business successfully. These factors might be related to keeping accurate records, keeping overhead costs low, maintaining a skilled and experienced work force, and so forth. Generally, these factors are not the targets of competitive intelligence information gathering, but they may be if they figure prominently in gaining or maintaining an advantage over one's competitors.

Environmental strategic keys influence all businesses. Some of these factors might be

- Legislation that affects your business adversely
- Government expenditure or taxation policies
- Environmental protection laws or regulations

These are factors over which you have very little control but that can make the difference between success and failure in business anyway.

Identify Your Strategic Keys

Identifying your strategic keys should be part of your strategic planning or thinking process. You could start by identifying your firm's strategic strengths and weaknesses and then developing action plans for either taking maximum advantage of your business's strengths or bolstering the weak areas. In making these judgments, management is basically identifying its strategic keys and deciding how to develop the strategic characteristics necessary to be less vulnerable to competition.

To start your own competitive intelligence research, prepare a worksheet like Table 7.1 that lists your own business's critical strategic keys and identifies the information you might require to maintain or build your strength in each factor.

As Table 7.1 illustrates, several factors might be critical strategic keys for an animal feed retailer, but the dominant factors are likely to be environmental and industry practices. In this case, there are many, many potential suppliers of feeds to this retailer, and those suppliers supply other markets as well. The products sold are largely commodity products. Although there are some very large suppliers, this is a business characterized by many small retailers.

This small business's major controllable factors are the prices of its products and the responsiveness of its personal service and delivery services to its customers. These items, therefore, are the focus of this firm's local competitive intelligence efforts.

WHEN IS COMPETITIVE INTELLIGENCE VALUABLE?

Unlike very large businesses, small businesses and entrepreneurs often face markets in which most strategic keys are not subject to their control. They can determine their pricing and service strategies, but they exercise little control over suppliers, product design, or the environmental or industry factors that influence the product or service they provide.

Economists would say that in markets characterized by many suppliers, many competitors, and many customers, a resaler will have very little control over any of the elements of its marketing mix. Products are commodities, and service is standard. Even the sales price is not subject to the control of the business because a price increase would simply send customers to all the other businesses and price reduction would cause a fall in profits.

To an economist, such a firm is a *price-taker*, and in such a market, competitive intelligence would be of very limited value. No competitor would be able to gain control of any portion of the market. There would be no competitor large enough or powerful enough to think strategically about.

But if one or more of your competitors have an advantage in any of the strategic keys for your industry, it becomes very important to understand those competitors' strengths and weaknesses, and conducting competitive intelligence research can be important to defending your own firm.

When a firm finds an unoccupied or protected market niche and has no close competitors, then competitive intelligence is almost entirely concerned with monitoring industry and environmental factors. Understanding and building strength in those factors might, after all, prevent a powerful competitor from entering your market niche.

A small town may have room for only one hardware store. A rural community may have room for only one grain silo. And in those limited markets, a firm can exercise some control over the price it sets, the products it markets, and the services it offers.

In larger towns, the size of the market will allow for more competitors. But those competitors may vary their offerings in significant ways to serve slightly different target markets. Even relatively small markets are segmented, and each segment responds to a slightly different marketing mix.

TABLE 7.1   Stategic keys for the animal feed business

Strategic key	Firm	Industry	Business Environment	Information requirements
1. Dependable supply of feed grains year-round		x	x	Feed grain crop forecasts by U.S. and state Departments of Agriculture
				Lists of potential suppliers in various parts of the country
2. Ability to acquire and keep stored grains free from mold, disease, or contamination		x	x	Directory of feed grain testing laboratories and state certification requirements
				Customer requirements identified in interviews
3. Competitive price	x			Prices being charged by competitors
4. Free delivery to customer barns/ farms/homes	x			Delivery services of competitors

Competitive capability				Information needs
5. Dependable unskilled, low-wage labor	x	x	x	Whom to contact to locate additional labor when required Minimum wage level What is the wage level paid by the competition?
6. Maintaining inventories for feeds for a wide variety of animals	x			What mix of feeds should be maintained for area animal stocks? What animal markets is the firm targeting?
7. Quick service	x			How quickly do competitors in my market area deliver agricultural feeds?
8. Dependability	x			Are customers satisfied with the dependability of delivery on time by competitors?

Think about your own town. One auto dealer may chose to set his prices relatively high and sell pricey luxury sedans to higher-income patrons. Another dealer may chose to sell used cars and sell most of those to middle- and lower-income families. Yet another entrepreneur may specialize in providing economical repair service after the sale to all these automobiles and thrive because of the higher-priced service facilities of the original dealers. All provide repair service for automobiles, but there is still a place for the businessperson who supplies economical auto repair because the cost of repair is a strategic key in the industry.

Although some businesses are satisfied with maintaining parity, others strive to gain a strategic advantage over their competitors. A program to gather and use competitive information in your decision-making process can be utilized for either purpose.

HOW TO GATHER COMPETITIVE INTELLIGENCE

The first step in preparing to gather competitive intelligence is to think through the process you will employ to collect it. What sources will you look to, and in what order will you proceed? There are no hard and fast rules about this process, but common sense will suggest some approaches to you. For example,

- Consult those persons most likely to cooperate with you first, such as employees, advisors, consultants, and members of organizations of which you are a member. Then look outside your own circle of contacts.
- If time is not extremely important, look to the free and low-cost alternatives first.
- Take advantage of free expertise and staff resources first.

Outside sources will, however, probably be your most valuable source of time-sensitive intelligence information. Consider contacting such sources as your competitors, customers, suppliers, industry consultants, security analysts, and middlemen in your distribution channel.

For outside (primary) sources, telephone networking is probably the lowest-cost and most efficient method to gather information. Your inquiries will, in some instances, be met with curiosity, suspicion, and objections, so think through exactly what you would like to ask, avoid direct questions that might be viewed as nosy or intrusive, have answers to objections you are likely to encounter, and be enthusiastic.

SOURCES OF INTELLIGENCE INFORMATION

Information on competitors is grouped into two categories:

- Published sources
- Nonpublished sources

Published Sources

Most of the sources of competitive information that the businessperson is likely to be able to access are published, or secondary, sources. Many of the published sources were identified in chapter 5, "Using the Library and Other Secondary Information Sources."

Today, "published" sources include those stored in electronic formats (on-line databases, CD-ROM, or magnetic tape) as well as on paper. They will have varying degrees of applicability to taking strategic advantage of close competitors. Some of the most relevant sources of intelligence data for smaller businesses will include

- Trinet—Sales, financial, and marketing data on businesses of 20 employees or more
- Electronic yellow pages—Directory listings by Standard Industrial Code classifications

• Dialogue—One of the best supermarket databases, which can be accessed on-line by anyone with a PC (and an account)

Consult *Gale's Directory of Databases* to locate the best on-line sources for your particular needs. However, as suggested in chapter 5, first try to determine whether library policy might entitle you to a free search of the literature. By this point, you should have selected your preferred reference libraries and become familiar with their policies regarding on-line searches for patrons.

In most instances, on-line databases will be more effective in uncovering past data on larger companies than recent data on very small companies. It is, however, a fast method of retrieving large amounts of information, so if quick access is critical, it may be worth it.

On-line database searches are expensive and can easily total $50 to $300 each. Moreover, if you are not experienced in using the database service, the cost in on-line time can be even higher. If you choose to try an on-line search, either get training or employ an information broker who knows the required databases and is an efficient user.

The library and on-line databases, however, are not the only sources of published information on your competitors, industry, and business environment. Some of the other published sources are

• Magazine or trade journal articles
• Association newsletters
• Industry newsletters
• The yellow pages
• Company credit reports
• Newspapers and want ads
• Government documents
• Industry analyst reports
• Filings with government or regulatory agencies
• Patent records
• Court records

Magazine or trade journal articles focusing on your industry will cover industry and environmental strategic keys for your business and will frequently profile large, successful competitors. Make it a habit to regularly scan these sources for general information that you can later use in your business planning.

Association newsletters are good sources of environmental information, especially pending legislation, economic news, resources available, and so forth. Ofttimes, these periodicals offer practical tips on marketing opportunities as well.

Industry newsletters survive sometimes because they can report news and information more quickly than the monthlies. Many newsletters have thrived over the years, for example, by interpreting government regulations to business.

The yellow pages is a practical tool for competitive intelligence for entrepreneurs and small businesses because in them your competitors announce the products and services they intend to market and sometimes spell out the advantages they think they have in the marketplace.

Company credit reports reveal all sorts of information about your competitors and are easy to access. Financial information, ownership data, and other general business data are stored right there for your study.

Newspapers are another major source of information on competition. Small businesses especially must try to take advantage of daily, and sometimes weekly, industry and competitor news sources. Not only do newspapers generally have reporters and editors assigned to cover local business news, but many also have business sections, want ads, and business staffs that work regularly with business groups. Moreover, your competitors, in their zeal for free advertising and publicity, will often issue press releases giving you notice of major events in their businesses. Consequently, one of the most valuable sources of competitive information you can have is a clipping service, as was mentioned at the close of the previous chapter.

If you have access to an Internet account or are a member of an on-line service such as CompuServe or America Online, you can subscribe to an electronic clipping service. Newspaper database services are some of the fastest-growing specialty firms in the on-line world. If you subscribe, each week you will receive many electronic newspaper clippings on topics that you chose (and pay for).

However, the national clipping services generally cover only the thousand or so largest newspapers. Small-town papers will not be covered, so you may want to consider doing your own "clipping" in newspapers from those towns in your market area not covered by your clipping service.

Government Files

Government documents are sometimes overlooked in the search for competitor information. Although tax filings are not available, many other government documents are in the public domain and can be examined. In the insurance and health care industries, state departments of insurance keep detailed filings of products and plans on file that are open to the public. The offices of secretaries of state maintain records of corporate filings and annual reports. Environmental protection agencies maintain development permits and land use studies.

Counties maintain court records, police records, and filings of proprietorship business licenses and property titles. State labor departments keep files on job-related accidents as well as labor problems and complaints. Better business agencies keep records of business complaints. If the business you want to study has issued stock, they will have detailed records on file with the Securities Exchange Commission. The list goes on and on.

The kinds of records you might want to review will vary from business sector to business sector, but there is information out there on nearly any company you might want to research. Almost every time a transaction occurs, a record of it is made somewhere.

If a proposal is submitted to a government agency, it is available for public examination after the bid is awarded, and that proposal will probably contain a great deal of important information on the proposing firm, including its financial status, officers, experience, and strategic strengths.

Industry analyst reports are sometimes another useful source of competitive intelligence. Watch industry magazines or journals, industry newsletters, and editorials for early notice of major events in your industry.

Nonpublished Sources

Small businesses are less likely to receive significant notice from the press than are larger ones, so you may not find many important notices about the strategic strengths and initiatives of your smaller competitors. All this means is that you may have to rely more upon nonpublished and primary sources of information for them than for your larger competitors.

Among the sources of nonpublished and primary data on competitors are the following:

- Your competitors
- Your engineering staff
- Brokers and business contacts in your competitor's distribution channels
- Your own salespeople and other employees
- Suppliers
- Advertising agencies
- Trade associations
- Conferences and professional meetings
- Speeches given by competitors' management
- Government contracts
- Competitor proposals to government agencies
- Building permits

- Local government maps, surveys, and property tax office aerial photographs
- Your customers

Your competitors are one of your best sources of information about their plans, capabilities, and intentions. In their efforts to communicate with their target markets, they will tell you much about their strengths and weaknesses. Whom do they perceive as their natural market? What is unique or superior about their product or service? Do they emphasize price, quality, or service? What image do they strive to create in the mind of the public?

Go to see your competitor's facility and keep your eyes open. Talk to the clerk about the store. How many people work there? Who is the owner? Who are the managers? Do they deliver? Is delivery free or is there a fee? What are the store's hours? Can they supply this or that? At what prices? What guarantee do they offer? Purchase several items that compete with your own key products and ask to have them delivered. As you leave, count the number of parking places and the number of cars in the parking lot. Check on the service you receive, on how fast your purchases are delivered, and on the condition of the delivery vehicles. Ask your investment broker for information (if it exists) on this company. And then ask yourself, how does your business compare?

If you have an engineering staff, have them take apart your competitor's product and give you an analysis of likely costs, strengths, and weaknesses. Ask them what the repair problems of the product are likely to be and how the product compares with your own.

If you sell through brokers, wholesalers, or retailers, ask them about the products, prices, and practices of your competitors. They will love to play you off against your competitor and will take great pleasure in slipping threatening information to you about your competition (and to your competition about you). You should understand that this is the nature of the world; *be careful* what you say and don't to say to these channel members. You probably need them worse than they need you for your business's success.

Train your own sales force to stay alert in the field to competitor activity and opportunities to obtain information. Competitor price quotes and product literature are often left at customer offices; overwhelmed by all the marketing materials, customers treat this material carelessly and discard it frequently. Salespeople are told about competitors' offers, service, and product features constantly. Provide your sales force with incentives for reporting this information back to the home office.

Your suppliers (and potential suppliers) are generally eager to curry favor with you in hopes of developing a loyal relationship. Take advantage of your position as buyer to ask questions about what other companies are doing and why.

Advertising agencies can be excellent sources of information on competitors, especially if they are handling your account. Many agencies are likely to have contacts throughout your industry and can make a few telephone calls to gather information if they feel it will ingratiate you with them. They will know personnel in the agencies used by your competition and will find opportunities to discuss your companies when they meet. If your business is an advertising agency, try talking to prospects about your competitors.

If you are a member of a trade association, pay a visit to your industry library and check out the materials on other companies. The librarian will have made a comprehensive literature search to accumulate as many materials on the industry and its members as you are likely to find anywhere.

Try attending conferences and professional meetings to gather primary information about your competitors. Speeches by industry experts may reveal previously unsuspected plans, new products, noteworthy reorganizations or management changes, success stories, or insights into future trends in the industry. Many an important fact has also been picked up in the bar after dinner when traditional competitors relax over a rum and tonic.

Speeches by competitors at local clubs and business meetings can also be a very useful source of detailed information on plans and activities. Traditionally, giving speeches to local business groups has been one of the most productive methods used by small businesses and entrepreneurs to establish relationships with potential customers and promote their businesses.

Does your competition have a contract with a local, state, or federal government agency? Visit that agency and ask to see their original proposal and contract. Normally you can gain access to these materials under the Freedom of Information Act. You will be surprised at the amount of financial and corporate information that the competitor must reveal to do business with the government.

Check out the files of the local building commission for competitors' building permits, and visit the local property titles office or planning department for maps, surveys, and aerial photographs revealing your competitor's property. Are records on health, fire, or safety inspections available on your competitors in local consumer protection agencies or health departments? Ofttimes, government inspector reports on visits to your competitors' establishments contain supporting information related to the size, work force, management practices, and design of competitor facilities.

Conduct a survey of your customers asking them for comparisons between you and your competitors, especially as regards your firm's identified strategic keys. Later on we'll deal with how to construct such a survey.

Have any of your employees worked for a competitor in the past? Ask them for help in understanding your competition. Conduct an interview with each one and cover issues of strategic or tactical importance. Ask your accountant to keep his or her eyes open for data on the financial performance of competitors. Ask your salespeople to look for information on the sales and prices of competing products and services and to talk with customers about their likes and dislikes for competing company products. Ask your legal advisor to watch for lawsuits involving your competitors. Do you employ a consultant? Ask him or her to keep you appraised of important information about your competition. Employees and consultants like to participate in bringing information to your attention because it brings them to your attention.

THE ETHICS OF COMPETITIVE INTELLIGENCE

Obviously, there is pressure on the searcher to engage in cloak-and-dagger methods to learn critical information about competitors. However, be warned that there are laws to protect business secrets, so avoid the temptation of untruths and stealing. There are plenty of legitimate ways to gather information without resorting to illegal methods—just be persistent and keep working at it. Every business must track its competition, and your competitors know this as well as you.

I can guarantee that your competitor is checking you out. That is the nature of competition.

PREPARING THE MARKETING PLAN | **8**

Your marketing plan contains the guidelines for all the marketing activities of your firm and/or product. If you review different expert sources' marketing planning, you will encounter numerous formats. Some will argue that the marketing plan should be extremely brief. (The briefest I've seen, for example, was no more than seven sentences long.) Other sources suggest far more comprehensive formats.

In this chapter, we'll examine a fairly comprehensive and descriptive format. A comprehensive planning process should probably occur at the beginning of a venture, if at any time, because it forces one to think through all aspects of the marketing program at probably the most vulnerable period in its life cycle. But the choice of format is truly up to the entrepreneur or business manager.

Subsequent to a business start-up, the marketing plan might be abbreviated to shorter formats. Even in these cases, however, a comprehensive marketing plan should probably be completed on an occasional basis to verify the assumptions and facts that are guiding the decisions of the firm.

WHY PLAN?

The entrepreneur or small business manager prepares a marketing plan for at least these four reasons:

- It forces one to think through the details of taking a product or business to the market
- It demonstrates to bankers and investors that you have clearly thought through what market you are targeting, what your goals are, and how you intend to achieve your goals
- It guides the actions of any marketing managers you might hire.
- It provides a criterion against which you can determine whether operations have been a success during the period covered by your plan.

A marketing plan can be prepared for

- A product line only
- A single product in a single market area
- A single market
- A single geographic area
- A general area of responsibility within the marketing function
- An entire firm

Most of the time in this book, an entire firm is the focus of the marketing plan. The reader is left to make the appropriate adjustments in the format and content if a different focus is desired.

STRATEGIC VERSUS TACTICAL PLANS

Most marketing plans have some components that are strategic in nature and others that are tactical. Although there is some debate about how to define the term *strategic*, I use it to refer to long-term goals and actions by the firm that will create or maintain a sustainable advantage over competitors. Thus, strategic goals give continuity to marketing activities from year to year, and they create strong positions that are difficult for competitors to dislodge. An example of a strategic advantage is possessing the lowest-cost position in an industry. Another strategic advantage might be having the best-known and most highly regarded brand name products. Neither of these advantages are achieved overnight; attaining them may require years of consistent effort to drive down costs, develop superior-quality products and service, and create the right image.

Tactical actions, on the other hand, tend to be shorter-term, less-critical activities that contribute to the attainment of an objective. One *Webster's Dictionary* definition of *tactics* is "the art or skill of employing *available means* to accomplish an end" (italics mine). For example, a tactical problem might be phrased like this: With a given budget and sales force, how might a company organize its sales activities to reach a sales goal? Compare this to a strategic question: How should a company distribute its products and services, and with what size of budget, to gain the greatest long-term advantage over its competitors?

Marketing plans can spell out short-term objectives as well as long-term ones. They name the activities to be conducted and sometimes leave the question of how best to conduct them to marketing management. But for the first-time entrepreneur, knowing the best way for a given activity to be conducted for his product in his industry is often critically important. So I recommend that marketing plans developed by entrepreneurs for their first business should include details for each activity defining exactly how they intend to execute it.

For small businesses that have worked out the best ways to execute their basic marketing functions, it is less important to include the how tos in annual marketing plans, but keep in mind that markets change over time, and it may be useful to include assessments of how the firm's marketing functions are executed to ensure that changes are made in a timely fashion.

ELEMENTS OF THE MARKETING PLAN

The marketing planning process attempts to ensure that the efforts of the marketer are directed at clear opportunities, that risks and competitor threats to targeting those opportunities are evaluated, that some measure of success has been spelled out beforehand, and that all the activities involved in the marketing effort are coordinated in achieving those goals. Some practitioners place their analysis of the competition in the business plan apart from the marketing plan; I prefer to include threats within the marketing plan.

In general, the components of a marketing plan include

- Identifying your marketing opportunities and problems
- Assessing any threats or risks associated with targeting those opportunities (such as your competition, environmental changes, technological changes, etc.)
- Setting and quantifying your marketing goals
- Describing how success against those goals will be measured
- Describing the strategies that you will use to achieve those goals

Sometimes left out are these subsequent steps:

- Describing how you will monitor achievement against plan objectives
- Describing how you will evaluate performance

The plan itself is the product of a four-stage planning cycle (Figure 8.1):

- Opportunity evaluation
- Planning
- Execution
- Performance evaluation

FIGURE 8.1   The Planning Cycle

This cycle is an ongoing process. Normally, it is repeated each year, with a new plan produced to guide the new year's activities.

The entrepreneur produces a marketing plan at his business start-up but should monitor performance against goals during the following interval, evaluate not only the activities but the original plan as well, and revise the plan to integrate into it what has been learned. The small business manager does the same thing but is simply past the start-up stage of his business. Both face the possibility that market opportunities will change as competitors move into the intended market, as products change, or as environmental conditions change. The marketing plan (and business plan) is a living document and should be modified even in midyear should events negate the assumptions on which it was based.

IDENTIFICATION OF MARKET OPPORTUNITIES

Marketing research is involved with each stage of marketing planning. For example, opportunity evaluation requires a creative examination of the broader marketplace with the objective of identifying profitable business opportunities.[1] Occasionally, opportunity identification occurs subjectively in the mind of the entrepreneur. As Daniel Burrus recommends in his book *Technotrends*, "give your customers what they would want if they knew they could have it." Such opportunities emerge from the process by which new technology is developed. This use of new technology can sometimes be planned.

Businesses sometimes direct their engineers to develop new technologies to increase productivity and lower costs. This is one form of the product development process. Occasionally, outside firms will license this technology from its patent holder, or executives will leave and take knowledge of it with them to form new enterprises. These new firms will then use this new technology to replace the old and in so doing will (hopefully) displace their competitors.

In other instances, an entrepreneur may recognize the potential in a technology developed for one purpose to solve a problem or displace a technology supporting an entirely different product. A device developed for the National Aeronautics and Space Administration (NASA), for example, could be acquired by a private business to develop new products of its own. Because the technology already exists, the key in opportunity evaluation is recognizing how it may be employed for other uses. But a literature search of the NTIS databases may be necessary to uncover the opportunity.

As a result of discovering these opportunities, the entrepreneur or business manager might

- Introduce new products or services
- Modify or improve existing products or services in some way
- Expand the product line or add new services
- Reposition the product or the firm
- Change the market segments or niche that the firm will target
- Modify packaging
- Introduce sales incentives
- Make revisions in promotional strategies or techniques
- Change pricing policies

In business, very little stays the same for long, so even if your marketing plan is 100 percent correct at first, it will become a poorer basis for correct action with the passage of time. Marketing research is one of the tools that entrepreneurs and small business managers might use to identify those opportunities. Some of the types of research studies that can lead to identification of new opportunities are

- Reviews of the literature for new technologies, new products, or product ideas which might be commercialized in ways other than originally intended
- Group and individual interviewing of potential customers and suppliers
- Market segmentation studies which identify homogeneous groupings of buyers within the total market
- Product positioning research, which maps the major product brands or competitors relative to one another so that gaps in the market can be identified

The latter two types of studies would be formidable methodologies for the average entrepreneur or small business manager to master and are best performed by a professional marketing researcher who is familiar with both the statistics involved and the software required for them. The first two methods, however, are within the capabilities of most businesspeople because they involve only (1) reviews of secondary sources via library work or on-line database searches or (2) the interviewing of informed people in the marketplace who recognize unmet needs.

MARKETING PLANNING

The process of marketing planning may be done entirely by the entrepreneur or by a team of managers within the enterprise. The end product is a written plan that describes the market opportunities to be targeted by the firm, defines the risks and market threats in doing so, sets marketing goals for the firm or product, and spells out the strategies to be utilized in achieving those goals. Marketing research and competitive intelligence play important roles in developing the information for the plan and in conducting the analysis of that information.

The Major Elements of the Marketing Plan

The major elements of the planning document are

1. *The statement of business purpose*: This is a statement defining where your company fits in the marketplace. It should answer the following questions:

   - What business are you in?

   - What types of products will you manufacture and/or distribute?

   - What customer needs will you fulfill?

2. *The situation analysis*: The situation analysis provides a fact base and analysis of those facts to support the goals, marketing programs, and budget set for the business. Included in the fact base should be

- *Annual sales history (in units and dollars) and projections of sales, net profits, and market share* for three to five years into the future

- *The market overview*: An analysis of market and sales trends/ events over the past several years that have influenced the firm's current sales, profits, and market share

  a. *Definitions of the markets in which your products and services will be or are involved*: How large is each in terms of units sold and dollar volume per year? What are the growth rates of each market? What is your percent share of each market? Which related markets are you not penetrating? And how are these figures changing over time? What do buyers want? (Describe the buying process.)

  b. *Market trends*: What important trends are occurring in the market environment that will impact your business?

  c. *Product or services descriptions*: Describe in detail your intended products and services that will be targeted at the above markets. Detail their strengths and weaknesses in meeting customer needs. Where do they fit in those markets, and why are they good enough to support your business?

  d. *Competition*: A directory of your competitors accompanied by descriptions of how their marketing mix (prices, products, promotion, and distribution) compare with your own. Describe the strengths and weaknesses of each. What are each competitor's sales, share of market, business trends, growth rate, future plans, and pricing?

e. *Customer service*: How do you compare in customer service with your customer's wants and to your competitors' service levels? Where do you need to improve?

f. *Product and services distribution*: Describe your product or service distribution network and its strengths and weaknesses in terms of reaching your customers. What kind of market coverage does this arrangement provide? What portions of your market are being missed? Which sales people are not producing well? Which sales territories are not producing well?

g. *Company image*: How do your customers perceive your company? Are those perceptions helping or hurting your business? What do customers like best about your business, products, services, and policies? What do they dislike? With which customers do you have the best relationship? With which customers do you have the weakest relationships?

h. *Customer communication*: Appraise your customer communication strategy, techniques, and comprehensiveness. Is your range of product and service communication brochures, flyers, and mailers complete? Are they easy and interesting to read? Is your communication plan consistent and constant? Do all customer letters, visits, and telephone calls receive prompt attention? How are complaints and warranty claims handled?

3. *Problems and opportunities*: Problems and opportunities should be identified and described in the analysis of your fact base. Here are some ways you can make those identifications:

Problems:

- Where you had an objective, look to see if that objective was accomplished.

- In attempting to implement last year's plans, were any bottlenecks encountered? Examples might include

  Staff turnover

  Running out of sales literature

  New government regulations

  Inadequate staff training

  Breakdowns in order fulfillment

  Will similar bottlenecks hamper this year's marketing efforts?

Opportunities:

- Does your market analysis reveal an underserved segment of the market?
- Does your competitor analysis spotlight a weakness that you can take advantage of?
- Do your product sales show that you are showing more strength in some markets than in others?
- Are market trends revealing an opportunity for new product introductions in some of your markets?

4. *Nonfinancial and financial objectives*: Objectives are the core of the marketing plan and should flow directly from your identification of problems and opportunities. Thus, there are two basic types of marketing objectives:

- Objectives directed at removing marketing problems
- Objectives directed at realizing opportunities

Your statements of objectives, however, should be preceded by the *assumptions* supporting them. Some potential assumptions might be

- No addition of major competitors to your marketplace
- No major technological innovations in competitor products

- No additional governmental regulations affecting your ability to do business
- No changes in the tax rates imposed upon your business
- No strikes or other events that would interfere with the supply of products to your business

Objectives should be written to be

- *Specific*; they should address specific products, markets, or geographic areas.
- *Measurable*; they should be quantified so that their achievement can be verified.
- *Time-specific*; they should have deadlines attached to them.
- *Realistic*; they should be realistic rather than too easy or too hard.
- *Achievable*; they should be attainable with effort.

5. *The marketing program*: In this section, you spell out *the strategic and tactical actions* that you and your staff will undertake *to achieve the objectives above*. In format, the marketing program consists of a list of actions that will be taken, the priorities among those activities, what the target of each action is, the specific staff who will be assigned to accomplish each action, and the deadlines attached to each.

- Each of the activities in your list is linked to a specific objective.
- Generally, the marketing program describes in detail the company and/or staff actions linking your target markets to the elements of the marketing mix:

    Product pricing policy

    Products and services offered

    Promotion and communication

Distribution arrangements

6. *The budget*: A financial report detailing the financial resources that will be allocated to support the marketing program and other company activities.[2]

Marketing Research's Assignments in the Marketing Plan

The marketing plan may also contain research goals and assign research objectives to be completed before further action is taken. Some of these assignments may be directed at verifying marketing opportunities that are only hypothetical, whereas others may be intended to correct deviations of actual sales from planned sales. A product test may be assigned to marketing research before action to take the product to the market is approved. A product test would measure the reception by a sample of customers to a new or redesigned product and evaluate the product's likely success in the market. Another assignment might be a study to identify alternative courses of action for correcting a product's sales decline.

Some research studies deal with tactical issues, whereas others address strategic needs. Clarifying the best target markets for the firm would clearly be a strategic research project. On the other hand, clarifying which is the most effective advertising concept before funds are approved to implement a new advertising program would address a tactical need. Another tactical study might involve an evaluation of the sales procedures being followed by salespeople to determine whether more effective practices or procedures might be implemented.

EXECUTION OF THE MARKETING PLAN

As the marketing plan is executed by marketing staff and salespeople, the role of marketing research moves into *monitoring* and *measuring roles.* The gist of this research involves collection of information on (1) how effectively some of the assignments in the marketing program have been carried out and (2) the impacts of those actions.

Some of the more common research tools used for these roles are surveys to measure

- Customer awareness and recall of advertising
- Trial purchasing or intent to make a trial purchase
- Repeat purchasing dispositions or intent to make a repeat purchase
- Attitudes of buyers toward a product and their reactions to using it
- Customer satisfaction with products and service

There are established formats for constructing these survey questionnaires. Examples of possible questions are included in a later chapter on survey design and measurement. But the two major categories of monitoring systems fall under the headings *marketing information systems* and *customer satisfaction monitoring systems.*

Marketing Information Systems

One approach to the monitoring and measurement role is implemented through the design and operation of marketing information systems. Such a system involves

- The design of data collection methods and instruments to meet certain monitoring and performance evaluation needs of the firm
- The creation of a marketing database and database management system to store, manage, report, and utilize the data, in various forms, to guide the implementation of the marketing effort

During the 1960s and early 1970s, marketing information systems became popular as a way to gather information that might then be used for management decision making. However, the inflexibility of large data systems on mainframe computers and the costs of updating them soon discouraged many businesses from continuing them.

These early systems were essentially *historical data management systems*, sometimes called *passive database systems*.[3] Experience with these systems quickly proved that it was not cost-efficient in many instances to collect, store, and update all that information just to provide unchanging management reports. The captured data in these systems was used to report only on the results of tactical sales activities. Today, some businesses continue to rely on their marketing databases for this purpose only—measuring the results of sales efforts.

Since the early 1980s, however, the costs of hardware and software have steadily dropped until today even one-person businesses can obtain inexpensive equipment for maintaining marketing information systems. Moreover, that same equipment can handle word processing, accounting, desktop publishing, secondary data searches via CD-ROM, on-line database searches, maintenance of different types of databases, and contact management, among others. Consequently, the overhead costs of equipment and software can be spread across many company functions.

Second, with the software and development application tools in place today for microcomputers, database managers have the ability to adapt their marketing databases as they evolve and to adjust them to changing conditions quickly. Purchase data can be electronically transmitted into databases via scanning equipment using bar codes, and databases can be enhanced with appended data from database vendors.

New ways of linking purchase data to identifiers (via buyers' clubs and store credit cards) are enabling more economical updating of historical information. In short, technology is providing a highly efficient, low-cost method of gathering information, bringing it into our marketing databases, modifying the databases, and generating output in the form of both reports and practical marketing initiatives—all with relatively little labor involvement.

Finally, stored marketing data is being increasingly used to provide guidance to the enterprise. As these demands have expanded, marketing databases have progressed through to marketing intelligence systems and even further to integrated business databases. We will discuss these higher-order systems later.

Monitoring Customer Satisfaction

During the 1980s, the Total Quality Management Movement initiated by W. Edwards Deming took on real momentum in the United States. Largely initiated in reaction to the success of Japan and Europe in penetrating U.S. markets and major declines in traditional manufacturing industries in the United States, the Total Quality Management Movement nevertheless had major impacts on the consciousness of U.S. industry about product and service quality issues. Quality control efforts under the guidance of Total Quality Management programs and interest in customer satisfaction caused many U.S. companies to refocus on the wants and needs of their customers.

Part of that customer orientation generated new interest in monitoring customer satisfaction on an ongoing basis. In too many instances, however, customer satisfaction monitoring was used as a tool of quality control rather than marketing. Firms monitored their customers' satisfaction with products and services without using the resulting analysis to drive their marketing programs directly. However, the recent successes of U.S. automobile manufacturers provides evidence that at least some major manufacturers may have learned their lesson.

EVALUATION OF ACTUAL RESULTS

The evaluation stage in the marketing planning cycle involves comparisons between actual and planned measures of achievement to determine whether the plan failed or succeeded. The resulting analysis may lead to a conclusion that implementation was flawed in some way or that the plan itself was flawed. At many enterprises, this stage is performed by operational staff, sales management, or even executive management during an annual planning conference, but the analysis performed is essentially a research function.

The results of the evaluation are subsequently used by management for updating the marketing plan. The revised plan is implemented, evaluated again after a second cycle of operation, and again revised. This process goes on and on, year after year, so that the marketing plan can be kept up to date and problems solved as the firm grows.

COMMUNICATING WITH YOUR CUSTOMERS

9

As you begin to implement your marketing plan, you will begin to notice that some things are working as you thought they would and some are not. Maybe the people you thought would buy from you do not. Maybe the products or services you thought would do best are not. Maybe the advertising you were sure would be effective is not. What do you do about it?

You could just take the successes you are realizing and continue to do the same thing. Or you might conclude that portions of your plan are inaccurate and set out to determine just what those errors are.

To do that, you might create a communications system that gathers information from your customers and prospects that tells you what they really want, how they view your products and services, and what they might suggest to you to improve your business.

HOW TO MAKE SURE CUSTOMERS COMMUNICATE WITH YOU

Businesspeople do quite a bit of thinking about how they can communicate with their potential customers, but relatively few include in their marketing plan how they intend to ensure that their customers and prospects will communicate with them. Some firms rely on their sales force to serve as that communications channel, but there are several problems with doing so:

- Salespeople are selected to be good communicators and influencers. Consequently, they may not be the best marketing analysts.
- Salespeople have a conflict built in to their jobs that can bias communications coming to management. That conflict stems from the fact that if they are not successful at selling, they can easily interpret the problem as something other than themselves: your price is too high, your products are not as good as competitors, your customers can't get credit, and so on. In fact, the marketing research function should probably be independent of the sales function because it might well be called upon to evaluate the sales force's performance.
- With experience, salespeople will absorb a great deal of information about customers and their individual wants and preferences. But sooner or later, salespeople also leave and take other jobs. And when they leave, they take all their knowledge and maybe a few of your customers with them.

You could use a professional marketing research firm to conduct a research project that would tell you what steps to take, but most entrepreneurs and small businesses cannot afford that option every time something goes awry. You might, on the other hand, devise a continuous monitoring system to gather feedback—a customer satisfaction monitoring system.

CUSTOMER SATISFACTION MONITORING SYSTEMS

During the late 1970s, a study conducted for the White House Office of Consumer Affairs found that for every customer who complains, another 26 are unhappy but do not complain. Moreover, each of those 26 tells an average of 10 other people about their dissatisfaction. Unhappy customers cost U.S. businesses billions of dollars of lost sales each year.

One way businesses might try to learn about customer dissatisfaction is to conduct a customer feedback survey. How many times have you entered a business and noticed a stack of customer complaint cards on the service counter (Figure 9.1)? Recently, I began to informally visit businesses near my home just to see what kinds of customer feedback surveys were in use. I made the following observations:

- Most businesses I checked with did not have any system in evidence for systematically getting customer feedback.
- Chains and franchises were likely to have some type of customer satisfaction card system in place, but the information requested from customers on these cards varied from no questions at all being asked (a card was available with lines to guide handwriting in case a customer wanted to write anything) to very detailed questions about product quality, cleanliness of store facilities, speed and friendliness of service, problems experienced, and comfort.

Occasionally, I will eat at a restaurant where the manager comes out onto the serving floor to talk with customers. Mostly, this amounts to "How are you enjoying your meal?" with a slap on the back and a smile. Only once in over forty years have I been approached by a manager during a meal and asked if he could interview me and my companions about our opinions on his restaurant. This occurred recently at a fast-food restaurant near my home.

MAX'S CONVENIENT STORE

CUSTOMER SATISFACTION SURVEY

Dear Customer:

Thank you for shopping at Max's Convenient Store. Because we care about your satisfaction with our products and service, we want to know when we fail to meet your expectations as well as when we do well. Please take a moment to complete this brief survey to let us know how we are doing. Just fold this self-adressed and postage-paid card in thirds, staple or tape, and drop it in a mail box. For our records, please include your name and telephone number in the space provided at the bottom of this page.

1.   How long have you been shopping with us?

        ❑ Just started   ❑ Less than 1 year   ❑ More than a year

2.   Do you shop with us often?

        ❑ Once or twice a week
        ❑ Once or twice a month
        ❑ Other: how often? _____

3   Do you find adequate parking space when you shop with us?

        ❑ Yes   ❑ No

3.   Do you find the products, product sizes and brands you like at our store?

        ❑ Yes   ❑ No

    If not, what products or brands would you like for us to stock? _____

5.   Please rate us on the following store features?

	Personal Service	Product Quality	Competitive Prices	Covenience
Excellent	❑	❑	❑	❑
Good	❑	❑	❑	❑
Fair	❑	❑	❑	❑
Below expectations	❑	❑	❑	❑
Very poor	❑	❑	❑	❑

6.   Are our sales people always courteous and professional?   ❑ Yes ❑ No

7.   Overall, how do you rate your shopping experiences with Max's Convenient Store?

    ❑ Excellent ❑ Good ❑ Average ❑ Below average ❑ Poor

9.   If any part of your visit to our store was unsatisfactory, we want to know about it. If any of your responses above indicated dissatisfaction, may we call to ask further questions about your experience and to determine whether we might make it up to you? ❑ Yes ❑ No

Name: _____   Address: _____

City: _____ Zip: _____   Phone: _____

Thank you for taking the time to provide this feedback to us. If we can be of further service, please call toll free 1 (800) 123-1234 for information or customer assistance.

FIGURE 9.1 A Customer Satisfaction Card

I want to tell you about that interview because it was so un-usual. He used a questionnaire and spent about five minutes writing down my answers.

He first asked for descriptive information about us and then moved on to ask about the perceptions we had gained of his restaurant's facilities, service, and product as well as our satisfaction with the restaurant:

- Was service as fast as it should have been?
- Were his employees friendly and did they act as though our business was important to them?
- Was our meal served hot?
- Did the food taste good?
- Was our table clean when we sat down?
- Was the temperature in the restaurant comfortable?
- Had we had occasion to inspect the cleanliness of his rest rooms, and if so, were they clean?
- Had we been offered drink refills?
- Did we feel that we had received good value for the money we had spent? Which did we feel were the best values on the menu? Which did we feel were not as good a value?
- Did we have any suggestions for him about service, food, or facility.
- Were we satisfied, and how satisfied, with our dining experience?
- Would we come back again?

Thanking us for our help, he presented each of us with a coupon for a free sandwich on our next visit to his restaurant.

WHY PAY FOR COMPLAINTS WHEN YOU CAN HAVE THEM FOR FREE?

There are essentially two approaches to asking for customer feedback. One approach is *passive* and is typified by the use of customer

satisfaction cards or surveys in lobbies, on tables, at service coun-
ters, or sent through the mail. Such methods place the responsibility for giving feedback to management on the customer.

Although offering such cards to customers can be viewed as a
gesture acknowledging the importance of customer feedback, in
fact it is a weak gesture. Unhappy customers are far more likely to
complain to a manager than to complete a survey. Moreover, some
customers prefer to discontinue their patronage rather than to confront a manager, and they say nothing about their dissatisfaction.
As a result, management receives far fewer complaints via the
cards than truly exist. Those turned in are not likely to express
concern about the more serious problems because those are ver-
bally expressed to managers. As a result, card-based systems may
fail as an unbiased monitoring device for facilitating customer communications. However, such systems are better than no system at
all! And they are better still when used in combination with a more
active approach for soliciting customer feedback.

In an *active* approach, management takes responsibility for securing feedback from customers. Although neither the passive nor
the active approach for securing customer feedback guarantees that
the feedback will be used in the decision-making process to make
the business better from the customers' point of view, the active
approach has clear advantages in securing relatively unbiased data
because the surveyor has more control over who provides the information.

THE VALUE OF A CUSTOMER

The value of a customer to your business is greater than her con-
tribution to your bottom line during her initial visit to your store.
In fact, most businesses rely upon *repeat business* from its customers
to survive. Direct marketing companies depend on repeat business
because they too often realize losses from their initial offerings
through the mail.

A great deal has been written within the marketing literature on how to stimulate repeat business. In fact, increasing the lifetime value of a customer stems from

- Increasing the proportion of customers retained
- Increasing the numbers of new customers referred to you by your existing customers
- Increasing average annual purchases by each customer
- Decreasing the costs of marketing
- Decreasing direct costs by modifying your distribution method[1]

Before my interview with the young manager at the fast-food restaurant, I probably patronized his restaurant twice a month. Afterward, I went once or twice a week. I obviously liked the food well enough before my interview to continue patronizing the store, but I did not view the store as attractive enough to eat there more often. Why did I increase my patronage after my interview?

A marketing professor would probably say that the manager had conducted *relationship marketing* in his interview with us. He had asked for our opinions. He showed that our opinions were valuable to him. He had immediately acted to correct any problems we had experienced. And he had asked us to come again. We left with a heightened opinion of the management, the store, the service, and the food.

The very process of actively seeking customer feedback, showing your customers that their opinions are truly important to you, and acting on their opinions is a powerful marketing strategy. It also provides an important way of enabling your prospects and customers to communicate with you.

Don Debelak, in his book *Marketing Magic*, argues, "People like to buy products and services from people and companies they like. . . . Customers want you to create some kind of relationship with them."[2] Debelak goes on to identify 14 of the reasons he says account for why people might buy from you rather than someone else:

1. Your product solves a problem that no other product solves as well.
2. The customer perceives your product or service to possess one feature or benefit lacking in others' products or services, and that feature is relatively important to him or her.
3. Some people feel your product or service works best.
4. Some people feel more comfortable using your product than others' products.
5. Some people feel that your product has higher quality.
6. Some people feel that your product is the lowest-priced or highest-value product.
7. Some people will buy from you because they like you or like the way you do business.
8. Your return policies, guarantees, and support are important to some people.
9. Your product or service carries a prestige image that some customers appreciate.
10. Your business offers a wider choice to customers.
11. Your business location is more convenient to some customers.
12. Some people will continue to buy from you from habit.
13. Some people will buy from you because you always have the newest or most innovative products.
14. You offer a product that makes people feel good about themselves or others, makes them look good in others' eyes, or offers a way of showing love or appreciation.[3]

Correspondingly, there are reasons people don't or won't buy from your business, reasons that are sometimes harder to get from your suspects. Debelak offers the following list:[3]

1. Business buyers may fear making a mistake in buying from you.
2. Some suspects may not have developed sufficient trust in you or your product.

3. Some suspects may perceive that your products or services are of questionable quality.
4. Your products or services do not address an important problem of theirs.
5. Some suspects won't think they need your product at all.
6. Many prospects are likely to have satisfactory relationships with one or more of your competitors.[4]

Finding out why potential customers won't buy from you can be critical for revising your marketing plans, but simply asking them won't always elicit the truth. A friend might confide in you that your products or services are not acceptable, but a complete stranger is unlikely to do so. Some customers react very negatively to "hard sell" approaches and quickly recognize salespersons' efforts to identify their objections. With no relationship to protect, many customers will simply provide an answer that you cannot get around. It is stressful for people to confront a salesperson with a statement such as, "I don't know or trust you."

One way to get at true feelings, however, is to offer them a confidential survey form and a gift if they will help you find out what your problem is. Notice that I said "your problem" because it truly is *your* problem, not the prospect's problem. You might offer a "10 percent off coupon" for the next visit to your store or something else. The important thing is that you are asking for valuable information that you must know. If it has value, be prepared to compensate your suspects for the discomfort and trouble you are putting them through. The survey form can ask those sensitive questions if carefully worded and protect the customer's anonymity.

Should you try to survey everyone who doesn't buy? No, probably not. But you might consider surveying every tenth person who comes by your business one day each week. Make the survey short and have an employee standing by the door ask prospects if they would complete a quick, anonymous survey for the store.

USE YOUR NORMAL CUSTOMER AND PROSPECTING CALLS TO GATHER INFORMATION

If your business requires you to go to your prospects rather than having them come to you, then your task of getting them to communicate accurately to you is more difficult. If you are a consultant for example, you may have to contact 20 prospects to get an appointment with one. If you are skillful, you might be able to identify the reasons that one appointment won't buy from you, but how about the other 19 who won't see you? That is a lot of missing information.

My own preference is to establish a bilevel database of information on suspects and prospects. *Suspects* are prospects you know little about and with whom you have no relationship. However, I want to identify a certain basic level of information that can be gathered even from them. Prospects are those suspects I actually get to see. In these longer meetings, I have a longer list of questions I'd like to have answered before I leave.

If you contact suspects by telephone, you might be able to gather a basic set of data if you incorporate your basic questions into your telephone script. Ask nonthreatening questions that cannot be interpreted as a sales pitch. One way I've found effective is to introduce yourself and ask if they would help you with a brief survey. I use scripts like the following:

> I'm Ed Hester, a marketing consultant in Raleigh, North Carolina. I'm trying to determine whether there might not be opportunities for me to help some of the firms in your area with their marketing needs. I understand that you are Firm X's director of marketing and can answer my questions about your own marketing program. Is that correct?
>
> A: Yes, but I only have a minute to talk.
>
> Okay, I'll make it quick then. As I understand it, Firm X produces cardboard packaging for package goods manufacturers.

A: That's right, but we have a major interest in plastic bag packaging as a result of a merger with Firm Y a year ago.

Oh, I didn't know that you had recently expanded into plastic bag packaging. I did some work with Firm Y in their plastic packaging business a year ago, so I know how competitive that business is. Have you seen any of the recent research about how offshore manufacturers have been targeting this business and are gaining market share stateside?

A: I haven't seen any of that research, but I am aware of the entry by firms in Britain and several Middle Eastern countries into our markets.

My own specialty lies in helping businesses improve the effectiveness of their marketing programs and profits in three ways: First, by developing an internal marketing research capability to identify problems and present possible solutions to managers like yourself. Second, by creating a database marketing capability that can bond customers to your company. And third, showing companies how to base their marketing communications on customer research from those two resources—marketing research and database marketing.

Do you have an in-house marketing research department?

A: Yes, of a sort. We have two analysts assigned to do in-house work for us.

How about a department of database marketing?

A: No, we don't have that.

Do you feel that your company's advertising program is taking currently available research into account in its appeals to the market?

A: I doubt that they do any research of any kind.

Have you ever used an outside consultant for Firm X?

A: Yes, occasionally. We use a firm out of New York occasionally.

Whom do you use?

A: XYZ International.

What have you found to be especially useful about its services? Have you been completely satisfied with the support you are getting?

A: XYZ is very good at finance. Our executive staff seems satisfied. XYZ doesn't do much work with marketing, however. I don't really know whether it does much work in the marketing area.

Are there any needs you have in marketing that might benefit from some outside help?

A: I don't know of anything that we need help with right now, but I'll be glad to let you know if anything comes up.

Can we arrange a time to get together to explore these issues further? I would be glad to spend half an hour with you at no charge or obligation to see if there is anything I could do to help. If not, perhaps I could refer you to someone who can provide the help you need. In the meantime, I will dig out a copy of that research report I mentioned and bring it to you. When we get together, we can talk about it.

In my telephone interviews, I try to build a consistent database of information. In the previous conversation, I've established the following points:

- The name, address, and telephone number of the director of marketing
- The size of the company, the industry, and major products being marketed
- New product lines being introduced
- That recent research is not known by the key marketing decision maker
- This company has an in-house staff doing marketing research and does not have an in-house database marketing unit. The director of marketing does not believe that customer research is being used effectively as a resource for planning advertising strategies.
- The company occasionally uses outside consultants to support its marketing efforts.

- XYZ International is the consulting company currently being used by this company.
- What about XYZ this prospect finds particularly effective
- This person is satisfied with the support received from my competitor.
- He does not recognize any unmet needs of his marketing program that he would trust to an outside consultant.
- The time and date of an exploratory meeting

For those suspects with whom you land an appointment, be prepared to identify and ask for additional information and to make that additional information a part of your database of information on prospects.

THE PARTNERSHIP OF MARKETING RESEARCH AND MARKETING

In this chapter, I've attempted to demonstrate that marketing without marketing research is as inconceivable as marketing research without marketing. They go together as complements and supplemental activities in the marketing process. Marketing without marketing research is one-way communication; it is salesmanship without listening to the customer. The real questions are how much marketing research should you do, who should do it, and what should be done—not *whether* it should be done.

In the next chapter, we turn to a technological approach to marketing and marketing research called database marketing. True believers of this science and art insist that database marketing is *not* marketing research but is a means of guiding the marketing effort based on building relationships with customers by giving them what they want and need. I will leave it to you to decide whether database marketing is marketing research or not.

MARKETING INFORMATION SYSTEMS

10

In our previous chapter, we examined ways in which a firm might begin to build monitoring systems that provide for regular communication of information from its suspects, prospects, and customers. This information is collected because it is useful in understanding the customer's wants, her view of the business and product offerings, and her willingness to do business with you.

Information can be kept informally in file folders, in the memories of salespeople, or in a structured computer database. Database marketers prefer the electronic media because of its advantages for integrating the research and marketing process.

STRATEGIC MARKETING DATABASES

Using a marketing database for guiding the marketing effort is one strategy for achieving these advantages for small businesses. If you collect the right types of information about your customers and prospects, these systems will not only monitor marketing activities but also provide continuous guidance for decision making.

Database marketing has two main purposes:

- Developing and maintaining a close relationship with customers
- Using the information contained in your customer database to improve your marketing to prospects[1]

It does this through studying the needs and behaviors of customers.

INTEGRATING RESEARCH AND OPERATIONS

The goal of systems based on consistent monitoring and database marketing is to *keep on plan by ensuring a constant flow of information from customers and prospects.* Unlike their more traditional cousins, the new marketing databases provide more than just research and monitoring of tactical goals. The occurrence of a communication from a customer or prospect triggers a quick marketing response by the firm. Because they can provide strategic guidance for the firm, database marketers argue that a marketing information system (MIS) pays for itself by preventing management errors due to ignorance of what is happening in the marketplace.

These databases go by different names in the marketing literature. Jackson and Wang, for example, in their book *Strategic Database Marketing,* identify three types of these databases that form, in their minds, a progression of increasing sophistication. The simplest and least-advanced form they call "historical data management systems," which are used primarily to track data captured from tactical marketing programs (such as a direct mail campaign). The next level of database they refer to as "marketing intelligence databases," which allow the marketer to analyze the data for detailed marketing decisions. The third and highest level of database marketing is referred to as "integrated business resources," which

contain financial, customer service, distribution, inventory, manufacturing, research, and marketing data.[2]

CONTINUE TO PROVIDE FOR
SPECIAL STUDIES

The MIS approach does not entirely eliminate the need for periodic
special studies because database design cannot possibly anticipate
all possible data requirements for analysis of marketing problems;
it can, however, anticipate many of the major information needs
because those are defined by the firm's and industry's major
success factors. Moreover, MIS systems can accommodate less-
structured or anecdotal data. The system developer's goal is to design these systems to have

- Provisions for holding enough information so that emerging
  opportunities or problems can be identified as they occur
- Provisions for enough data to be held in the database so that
  the sources of those opportunities and the causes of those problems can be identified with a high probability

If necessary, special studies can then be initiated with much
lower information requirements than would be necessary if no MIS
data were available. Possibly these additional data can be found in
secondary data sources or through anecdotal research methods.

DEFINE YOUR INFORMATION NEEDS

Data requirements for a marketing information system will depend
upon the objectives set for it:

- Step 1: Define who in your organization wants information
  from the database and what they intend to do with it.

- Step 2: Consolidate these wish lists and eliminate low priority requests.
- Step 3: Define the data requirements to meet each of the remaining objectives.

Arrangements to gather these data can be organized by identifying all the ways a business already communicates with its customers. For example, some of those communications might include service contacts, telephone orders or point-of-sale contacts, direct mail promotions, product queries, newsletters, warranty cards, and customer satisfaction response cards. Each of these communications channels can be designated to collect a portion of the total data requirements.

Arrange to gather your desired information from *appropriate* communication, however, and use approaches that make sense to customers or prospects. When completing service or repair on a product, for example, a customer will expect to be asked certain questions about use, age of the product, and identity but may find your request to provide details on the model and year of his car irrelevant.

IDENTIFY METHODS TO RETRIEVE THE DESIRED DATA

To build a database, the firm will need to develop its own methods to gather information not readily available from its normal internal sources:

- Surveys of customers and prospects
- Research panels
- Prospect list development projects
- Customer referral programs

Data gathering has a cost, and each data field to be gathered should be evaluated against the cost of gathering it. Gathering the data and keeping it updated is obviously a multiyear commitment. Even if additional fields are not added, the database will grow owing to the addition of transactions data as prospects are added, customers repeat purchases, new promotions are run and responses are recorded, and new products are added.

AUTOMATING YOUR FILING SYSTEM

Internal Sources

Most businesses keep files of some kind on their customers. These files are said to be *internal data sources*.[3] Because the business controls its own gathering of this type of data, it can decide how comprehensive it wants its files to be and arrange to have its own staff collect it. Faced with a need to create a marketing information system, businesses can minimize their expenditures by shifting more of the data collection to internal sources rather than external.

Examples of customer data commonly collected by firms for these databases might be

- Customer identification code, name, title, and address
- Sex, age, and income
- Lengths of residence and size of household
- Acquisition source and date
- Telephone number
- Purchase history, offer exposures, and offer responses
- Sources of orders and amounts of transaction
- Payment methods
- Products purchased

Business-to-business database fields might include

- Company identification code, name, and address
- Buyers' names and titles
- Influencer names and titles

- Industry classification (SIC codes)
- Business size: revenues and number of employees
- Channels used in ordering
- Offer exposures and response history
- Purchase history

Although the entrepreneur starting out might keep his few records in a manual filing system, at some point in the growth of a business, it will become more efficient to transfer those manual records to a computer database. The database would need the capability to enter the required fields, generate reports, and execute a number of operational tasks.

External Sources

Even small businesses can supplement their internally gathered source data with purchased data from a variety of sources. One type that can be purchased from outside commercial sources is *demographic data*. This type of data can be purchased from many database/list companies. In most instances, however, demographic data can be gathered for the firm by salespeople or through company surveys, credit application forms, and credit reports. Demographic data includes such measures as

- Home ownership
- Number, names, and ages of adults in household
- Number, names, and ages of children in household
- Birthdays
- Occupation
- Income
- Length of residence

A second type of commercially available data is *lifestyles data*. Vendors develop statistically defined market groupings of individuals or families in predefined lifestyle categories. Examples of these lifestyle categories might include

- Those interested in reading books
- Those interested in wines
- Owners of horses
- Golf enthusiasts
- Craftspeople
- Fishers or hunters
- Boat owners
- Bicyclists or runners

This data may be leased in the form of electronic files containing lists of individuals plus the above data fields. Individuals on these lists can be matched to your own list electronically to add to your customer and prospect information.

Yet another example of purchased data are the so-called *behavioral indicators* of consumer financial status, buying activity, or attitudinal patterns. Individual businesses, however, can often collect this type of information directly from the customer or prospect:

- Mail-order buyers of various types of products
- Donors or patrons
- Credit card users
- Purchasers of stocks and bonds
- Makes and models of automobiles owned

The leasing of new lists of mail-order buyers for your type of product might be an important enhancement to a mail-order business. It can significantly expand the number of customers and repeat customers.

Finally, data developed from statistical "marketing segmentation models" can be leased and overlaid on a business's own data. For obvious reasons, these data are referred to as modeled data." Examples of segments used essentially as additional lifestyle identifiers might include

- The Aristocrats
- Wealthy Intellectuals
- Country and Cowboy
- Upwardly Mobile
- Retirees

For large merchandisers, the leasing of these data makes good economic sense sometimes, but modeled data are expensive for the small business. Moreover, other single variables might be good enough for defining market segments, especially because small businesses are generally "closer" to the customer and might even know every customer personally. For example, knowledge that husband and wife are retired and middle income may be sufficient for you to satisfactorily define their buyers' grouping.

WHY COLLECT ALL THIS INFORMATION ABOUT SUSPECTS AND PROSPECTS?

Our goal as marketers is to identify suspects, convert suspects to prospects, and convert prospects to customers. It is that simple. For low-dollar purchases, buyers may pass through that transition very quickly. Customers do not go through that transition quickly for major purchases.

Business managers have the task of guiding prospective customers through that transition, and the way they do that is to overcome prospects' reasons for not buying, to present to them as many reasons for buying as are necessary, and by asking them for the sale. This is really all they can do.

What role does all this information play in that task? *The information is the suspect's, the prospect's, and finally the customer's communication to us telling the business where he or she is in that continuum.* And then, once he or she becomes a customer, the information requirements shift to tracking his or her contentment with you, your business, and your offer.

That is all database marketing is about. As Arthur Hughes notes in his book, *Strategic Database Marketing*:

> If you want transactions to happen, you must find out what the buyer considers profitable. It may not be a low price; it may be better service, information, reliability, higher quality, helpfulness, friendship, or simply personal recognition. Each buyer may have different subjective values. By discovering each buyer's personal requirements, you can better fill these and complete more transactions. In the process, you will make your customers happier, keep them buying for a lifetime, and make your company profitable.[4]

WAYS TO USE YOUR MARKETING DATABASE

You will want to use your marketing database to

- Track your customers' patronage of your business
- Protect your relationship with them
- Increase the frequency and amount of sales to them

Here are some ways you might do that:

- Market a "store credit card" to customers or maintain records that link specific purchases to individual customers. This data will allow you to record which items are purchased by each customer over time, which then becomes part of your marketing database.
- Learn more about each customer's likes, dislikes, and demographic and psychographic profiles through surveys and appended data.
- Follow up customer purchases with special personal services—thank-you letters, follow-up surveys, and telephone calls—and becoming specialists in customer service.
- Keep track of birthdays, anniversaries, and other key personal events in customers' lives and communicate one-on-one when

they occur, so that your firm can become a family friend, not just another store.

- Use these data to analyze how to expand to other potential market areas and identify needed changes in products, services, facilities, management, marketing strategies, and sales tactics.

DEVELOPING A DATABASE MARKETING STRATEGY

Making best use of your marketing database requires an effective communication strategy. Consider the series of actions based on data entered into your marketing database that is shown in Table 10.1.

Database marketing is intended to make and keep a targeted group of customers through maintaining communication *both ways*—from the customer/prospect to the business as well as from the business to the customer. Now let's look at some of the major ways you can utilize your database.

1. Use your MIS to profile your best customers and analyze those profiles. Two ways to create these profiles include:

    - *RFM Analysis.* One technique for identifying your best customers is called recency, frequency, and monetary analysis (RFM). If you design your database to track individual customer transactions, you will be able to:

        Report how recently each customer has made a purchase from you[5]

        Compute the average expenditure by each customer and how the amounts of those expenditures have changed over time

        Compute the number of times each customer has made a purchase from you

TABLE 10.1   Example of a database marketing strategy

Timetable	Planned actions
New customers:	
10 days after first purchase	Mail a thank-you note and a follow-up survey about satisfaction and other needs.
4 weeks following first purchase	Send a "We have missed you" note.
6 weeks following any purchase	Have a salesperson call and offer a discount on any purchase.
12 weeks following any purchase	Survey for customer satisfaction. Include a discount coupon.
Prospective customers from a purchased mailing list:	
As soon as you obtain a name	Send a personalized letter and a short-form catalog.
10 days after first mailing, if prospect hasn't become a customer	Follow up with telephone call by salesperson, offer a discount coupon, and extend invitation to come by store.
3 weeks after telephone call, if prospect still hasn't become a customer	Mail a survey form with personalized letter asking for reasons for the lack of response and a bigger discount coupon.

- *Comparison Analysis.* If you do not chose to incorporate customer transaction data into your marketing database, you can still do comparisons between your "best" customers— however you may chose to identify them—and all the rest of your customers.[6]

Identifying the best customers will be an important use for your marketing database. Because your best customers clearly prefer you and your services or products, you can hold down marketing costs while maximizing customer response by promoting primarily to them. Other customers are less likely to respond to your offers, but it will cost just as much to send promotions to them.

With your existing customers, and especially your best customers, you will want to utilize a retention marketing strategy in all your communications to defend your customer base from your competitors. Your objective with this strategy is to offer them value, which will limit your risks of losing them to competitors.

Based on your research on your existing customer base, many other options open to you for gaining new customers or converting existing customers into more frequent buyers, for example, Jackson and Wang suggest the following strategies:

2. Market to Suspects and Prospects. In database marketing, marketers use one of two approaches for prospecting: (1) Seeking lists of prospects whose profiles mirror the profiles of your best customers and (2) identifying your competitor's customers.

    - *Find New Customers Who Look Like Current Best Customers.* List companies will lease lists of individuals or businesses to you, but the demographic data they maintain may not be sufficient to define an appropriate list of prospects. Large database marketers will enhance list data with additional purchases of demographic and lifestyle data. The technical expertise to execute this process in many cases may be too complex for most entrepreneurs or small business managers, but it can be managed in some cases with the support of a database marketing consultant.

    - *Identify Competitors' Customers.* Through the use of surveys, even the small business can gather information from prospects on their use of competitor products, competitor prices, product strengths, and their relationships with competitors. For these prospects, a business can execute a promotion to entice them to try his products and then build new relationships. These promotions are called "switch strategies."

Direct mailings are a favored method for these promotions because they may not be noticed by your competitors. If they are noticed, competitors may respond quickly with defensive promotions. However, major players may not care whether their efforts are noticed because they feel they have a product advantage and their terms of sales prevent switching back. The major software houses, for example, are using switches when they advertise that they will grant upgrade prices to new users when they switch from competitors' products.

- *Deliver a Message Consistent with Product Usage.* This use of database information utilizes strategies to move infrequent purchasers along towards heavy purchasers. The objective is to make every customer into a "best customer."

- *Reinforce Purchase Decisions.* Communicate with your customers after they make purchases to say thank you and to congratulate them on making a good decision.

- *Cross-sell and Encourage Complementary Purchases.* Every person or business purchases a wide variety of products daily that fits their needs or operations. Likewise, a given customer profile will be receptive to a large number of products and services that fit specific needs or operations. For example, all new parents are likely to have a need for many different products associated with having a young child in the house. Cross-selling involves offering your best customers complementary products and services that fit their lifestyles, needs, or operational requirements. Complementary purchases occur when products and services that do not fit a customer profile are repackaged or modified in some way to make them a better fit.[7]

GETTING STARTED

Obviously, initiating a database marketing program involves an investment of time and money, but for many businesses, the investment in learning the technology and the methodology is probably the most critical. It is very likely that a business will need, and purchase, a personal computer or establish a network of computers anyway, as well as software necessary to support a marketing database.

For more details, buy a good book on how to do database marketing. Two of my favorites are

Arthur M. Hughes, *Strategic Database Marketing* (Chicago: Probus Publishing, 1994).

Rob Jackson and Paul Wang, *Strategic Database Marketing* (Lincolnwood, IL: NTC Business Books, 1994).

TACTICAL RECORD KEEPING IN THE MIS

In spite of the emphasis these days on strategic database marketing, don't neglect the record keeping needs of your sales force. Sales management will require reports from the MIS on salesperson performance. A database should include fields to identify salespersons, dates of sales, sales revenues, and product identifiers.

The sales history required for forecasts and the marketing plan must come from this database, and forecasts of sales into future years will probably be based on historic sales reports. Marketing objectives and individual salespeople's quotas will also be set based on these data.

Sales management will expect to receive a set of standardized reports on product and corporate sales by product, by geographic region, by salesperson, by month, and by many other sorts. This data will then be compared to sales goals or quotas and used in performance reviews with individual salespeople. Although these are tactical needs of the firm, they are nevertheless important.

CONDUCTING SURVEYS

11

If you are going to do your own marketing research, sooner or later you will need to collect *primary data*—data that is not available from existing sources.

You can collect primary data in three ways: observation, surveys, or interviews. With observation, you watch customer, prospect, or competitor behavior and describe or take measurements describing that behavior. Consider observation as a method for conducting some competitive intelligence research as well as for interviewing.

USING SURVEYS IN MARKETING RESEARCH AND DATABASE MARKETING

In marketing research, surveys are used for (1) marketing planning, (2) marketing problem solving, and (3) monitoring the marketplace. However, during the past 15 years, telephone surveys have become more difficult to implement owing to refusals to be surveyed, hang-ups prior to completion of the survey, and telephone answering machines. Public suspicion has been intensified by the practice of some telemarketers disguising their sales efforts as surveys.

In database marketing, surveys are used not only to gather information for research and other purposes but also to facilitate part of the dialogue between buyer and seller. So long as the information provided benefits the buyer, he is generally far more willing to share other data that helps the seller to understand those wants. It is up to the seller to make the buyer believe that he is interested in what the buyer really wants.

CAN THE SMALL BUSINESSPERSON DO HER OWN SURVEYING?

A variety of skills are needed to conduct a viable survey. The researcher will require the skill to design a well-constructed questionnaire.

In database marketing, surveys are generally administered by mail. Questions may be structured or unstructured, and the purpose of the survey will be undisguised. The nature of the survey's targets is determined by study of the marketing database and/or mailing list characteristics. This database analysis requires computer, analytical, and programming skills that must be developed through schooling, practice, and experience.

Marketing research survey projects require more choices and a somewhat different range of technical skills than database marketing campaigns. Although some questionnaires are designed to simply monitor customer perceptions—such as customer satisfaction surveys—most are constructed to gather data to evaluate different possible causes of a marketing problem and to evaluate the appropriateness of alternative strategic or tactical initiatives.

There is, in these instances, a structure within the questionnaire that may not be obvious to the respondent. In fact, some objectives of the questionnaire are likely to be disguised from the respondent to avoid biased responses. The inexperienced researcher may have more problems developing an appropriate survey format if her objective is something more than simply opening lines of communication with her customers.

A marketing research survey may be administered by telephone, mail, or personal interview. Because of the expense of conducting surveys by personal interview, this option is used in a relatively small number of research projects. Telephone surveys have some cost and speed advantages over mail surveys for professional telesurvey firms, but those advantages may not accrue to inexperienced and unsupervised telephone interviewers. Because of the inexperience factor, mail surveys may be a preferred choice in some instances even though they take longer to complete.

Marketing researchers need unbiased samples for their surveys in order to capture a representative portrait of the marketplace. Thus, statistical skills are required to select a random sample and determine the necessary sample size for the study. Further, statistical analysis of survey results may involve statistical testing, use of statistical software, and interpretation of the results—all technical skills not generally found among the general public.

Rather than maintain in-house research staffs, large corporations have increasingly contracted their research projects. This has allowed them to cut their costs while still having access to those skills when they are needed.

Small businesses, however, are able to do much of their own research, and for those tasks that require technical skills not available within the firm, a local consultant can be used to fill the gap for missing skills.

AVOIDING BIASED SURVEYS

Because surveys completed by a single business's customers are not likely to be random samples from the population of potential buyers, they tend to produce a biased portrait of the marketplace. In this case, *biased* means "not representative of the total potential customer population." Having a biased response may not represent a major problem for some marketers. Database marketers, for instance, are not really interested in obtaining a representative sample of their community. They want to focus on their best customers, whom they identify through analysis of their internal marketing databases. This knowledge guides their marketing efforts in a communications strategy designed to generate repeat business and seek new buyers. Marketing research pursues the same goal by seeking unbiased samples of the market.

SURVEY PURPOSE

A survey's purpose guides the content and construction of the questionnaire. Here are some typical purposes, but there will be many other legitimate ones:

- To measure market awareness of an advertising campaign
- To initiate or maintain communication with customers or prospects
- To determine how satisfied a business's customers are with its service or products
- To measure market shares of a business and its competitors
- To understand why customers have switched their patronage to a competitor
- To obtain descriptions of a business's strengths and weaknesses
- To assess how well a product or service matches the wants of a business's best customers

- To understand why infrequent buyers are not more frequent buyers

There is no reason why a survey cannot be used to strengthen the relationship between a customer and seller regardless of whether it is being used in a database marketing program or a marketing research project. The characteristics of a good survey are the same for either case.

SAMPLING FRAMES

A *sampling frame* is a comprehensive list of people, businesses, or organizations from which you intend to select a sample. All of the persons or organizations making up your market of interest are referred to as the *population*. The subset of persons or organizations selected for surveying is termed the *sample*.

Database marketers who intend to survey their best customers will pull their sample from their marketing database by selecting for most-frequent or highest-dollar purchasers. In this case, the list of all the business's customers serves as a sampling frame. Surveys are sent to a carefully defined *nonrandom* selection from that list.

A business that decides to do a customer satisfaction survey might draw a *random sample* of its own customers and send the surveys to them. If a marketing database contains 100,000 customers, a marketing manager may see no reason to survey them all and will instead survey only a small representative sample of those customers.

A business that wants to survey its competitors' customers might purchase a mailing list from a *list broker* and delete all of its own customers from that list. A management consulting firm that provides services to associations might seek the directory of associations at its local library. In short, the sampling frame you select should reflect your purpose for conducting the survey.

To do a survey by mail, you must have a list of the appropriate names and addresses. To do a telephone survey, you must have a list of the appropriate telephone numbers. Although there are techniques for doing random telephone surveying when you do not have specific telephone numbers, the entrepreneur or small business manager will generally do better to define a sampling frame from which to select his sample. Depending upon just who the subject of your intended survey is, your sampling frame might come from your own firm's records, from the phone book, from directories available at a local library or on-line database, from membership lists of an industry association, or from a company that leases mailing or telephoning lists.

RANDOM SAMPLES

If a questionnaire is sent to the entire population of interest, then you have all the information about that population that is available. You have not sampled the population, so your results, if all questionnaires are returned or completed, are complete.

When you sample, however, you survey only a portion of all the members of your population. Therefore, you have to worry about whether the measures you want from the sample are good estimates of the population. To get good representativeness, you must select a large enough sample, and you must use a random procedure for selecting elements from the population for your sample.

Sampling is a complex subject and cannot be covered with any justice in this book. However, with a little help, you can draw a simple random sample that will provide a good representation of your population of interest.

One simple method to draw a random sample is to find a table of randomly generated numbers at your local library, pick a starting point on it, and start selecting sets of numbers as you progress down a row or across a column. Random number tables are formatted something like Figure 11.1 except that you are likely to find full pages of these numbers.

If your sampling frame (list of population members) numbers 9,000 business names, for example, you might use groupings of four random numbers to select your random sample from among your numbered population elements. If you started on the second row in Figure 11.1, your first three sample members would be 7,740, 2,744, and 1,466. Your first three sample members would be the 7,740th, the 2,744th, and the 1,466th person, business, or organization in your sampling frame.

You would continue across that row, selecting groups of four random numbers. Upon reaching the end of the row, you would start back at the beginning of the next row and progress across that row, and you would continue this process until you reached the desired sample size.

Even for a simple random sample, however, one has to determine just how large a sample is required to have any confidence in the survey measurements. I suggest that you seek assistance in solving that problem from a college statistician or a marketing research consultant. In most cases, this task will not be time consuming or expensive.

Another procedure commonly used to select simple random samples is called *systematic sampling*. Systematic samples are especially useful for obtaining representativeness when your population shows systematic cycles or possess ranges of observations that are noticeably different than other groups. Housing patterns, for example, might have geographic clusters of low-income homes and other clusters of higher-income dwellings. A systematic sam-

17 46 85 09 55	17 75 64 34 55
77 40 27 44 14	66 25 22 91 48
91 48 23 68 52	11 27 35 41 92

FIGURE 11.1   A Block of Random Numbers

pling procedure should ensure that all such clusters have an equal opportunity of being included in a sample.

Let's assume that your marketing consultant has recommended that you survey 300 households. There are 3,000 households in the geographic area you want to survey. You will be sampling households from a telephone book that is organized by street address.

Because your planned sample size is 300, your sample will be one-tenth of the population size. You can take a systematic sample by using a random number table to select the first observation from your population list from among the first ten households listed. Beginning with that first observation, you would sample every tenth household as you progressed down the list.

Some surveys may require more complex sampling designs to obtain a good representation of a population. In these instances, seek advice from a qualified statistician.

HOW TO ORGANIZE YOUR SURVEY QUESTIONNAIRE

Experience over the years by both market researchers and database marketers has created some general rules guiding how to structure a survey form. Here are some of the more important of those rules:

- Make your mail survey professional looking. If it's longer than one page, make it into a booklet and include a cover letter explaining who you are and why your survey is important.
- Make your survey interesting to the respondent. A good survey will be fun and informative for the respondent to complete.
- Detail your instructions for completing the survey right at the beginning of the survey form. Briefly explain the purpose of the survey, why it is important, and assure the respondent of the confidentiality of his answers.
- Ask screening questions immediately after the instructions. *Screening questions* help the respondent to determine if he or she

is the intended respondent or if someone else in the home or office should answer it. Answers to screening questions also inform the researcher who completed his survey. For example, one screening question might read something like this:

> This survey should be completed by the individual in the household who makes the decisions about purchasing health insurance for the family. Would you say that
>
> *Check your answer:*
> ☐ You make the purchasing decisions for your family.
> ☐ You share the purchasing decisions for your family.
> ☐ You influence the purchasing decisions for your family.
> ☐ Someone else makes the purchasing decision for your family.
>
> *If someone else makes the purchasing decision for your family, would you please pass this survey to that person for completion? Thank you!*

- Ask general questions first. These are easier to answer and help to focus the respondent's attention on the detailed questions to follow. The first general questions in a questionnaire are often open-ended questions, which do not specify the possible answers, so the respondent can write anything he wishes in the space provided.
- Ask nonintrusive questions during the first part of the survey. Ask intrusive, emotion-charged, or sensitive questions last. Try to show by the logical flow of questions why the sensitive or emotion-charged questions are being asked at all.
- Make the order and flow of questions in your survey logical. Marketing researchers use what is called the "funnel approach" to shape the logic of questionnaire design. In the funnel approach, broadly worded and answered questions are positioned at the beginning of the survey, and very specifically worded and answered questions are positioned at the end.
- Ask nonconfrontational questions first and confrontational questions later. Asking "What did you like about our products? should precede "Why didn't you buy our products?"

- Break complex questions down into several simple questions. A so-called double-barreled question is a question, for example, that calls for two answers at the same time. Ask two questions instead.
- If subsequent questions depend on the answer to a preceding question, set up "skip patterns" by directing respondents to the next appropriate question. For example,

  ☐ Yes; if you selected *yes*, go directly to question #12 now.

  ☐ No; if you selected *no*, go directly to question #13 now.

- Select simple words in expressing your questions or providing instructions. Many adults in the United States function at only third- to sixth-grade reading levels. For example, use *gasoline engine* instead of *internal combustion motor*.
- Avoid asking questions that might call for estimates or guesses by the respondent. For example, avoid such questions as "How many long-distance telephone calls did you make last year?"
- Avoid confusing wording like, "Do you oppose legislation that would permit wide trailer access to our roads?"
- Avoid leading questions, for example, "Do you feel that abortions, which are killing millions of innocent children each year, should be outlawed?"
- Ask for classification information last; for example, demographics (age, sex, race), income and wealth, diseases and health problems, and other socioeconomic descriptors are used for classification purposes. These types of data will help you to understand differences in motivations, awareness, behavior, and attitudes across different economic and demographic segments of the population. Also, explain why you are requesting this type of data.
- After the final question in a mail survey, provide instructions to the respondent for mailing or returning his responses. In the event that respondents have questions about your meaning in some questions, provide an 800 number for them to call for clarifications or additional information.

STRUCTURED VERSUS UNSTRUCTURED QUESTIONNAIRES

Structured Surveys

Questionnaire structure refers to the amount of standardization designed into a questionnaire. In a structured questionnaire, the questions and answers are worded precisely the same for every respondent and presented in exactly the same order. Figure 11.2 is an example of a structured question.

With structured questions, each respondent hears or sees exactly the same question and chooses from the same set of possible answers. Where the possible answers to the questions are presented to the respondent, they are also referred to as *fixed alternative* questions.

Fixed alternative questions can be *dichotomous* or *multichotomous*. Dichotomous responses have two choices only. For example, questions that must be answered by Yes or No are dichotomous. Questions that request the respondent to identify their sex (male or female) are also dichotomous.

Multichotomous questions have more than two answer choices. The question in Figure 11.2 about the number of cups of coffee drunk each day is multichotomous because it has six possible responses.

On average, how many cups of coffee do you drink each day?
- ☐ No cups
- ☐ 1–2 cups
- ☐ 3–4 cups
- ☐ 5–6 cups
- ☐ 7–8 cups
- ☐ More than 8 cups

FIGURE 11.2　Structured Survey Question

Structured questionnaires have the advantage that they help eliminate differences in interpretation by respondents for what is being asked. Fixed alternative questions are best used where possible responses are well known, clear cut, and limited in number. They are especially appropriate for soliciting factual information (for example, years of school, age, sex) but are sometimes used to collect information on attitudes, awareness, and behavior as well. They are not very appropriate for soliciting information about people's motivations.

Unstructured Surveys

In an unstructured questionnaire, the purpose of the study is clear, but the alternative responses to each question are left open. The object of such questions is to get respondents to openly discuss their ideas, attitudes, opinions, and feelings about the subject. Subsequent questions by an interviewer then depend upon exactly what the respondent says in her initial, and then subsequent, responses. Unstructured surveys might be used, for example, in experience surveys or in focus group interviews to explore motivations or feelings about a business or product.

WHAT SHOULD BE MEASURED?

Surveys are used to measure a variety of concepts of interest. Among these are

- Awareness or recognition
- Attitudes and opinions
- Buying or nonbuying motivations
- Explanations of purchasing and use behavior

To measure these concepts, responses must be arranged so that *numbers* can be associated with each response. Because of that, we need to take a few moments to examine the topic of measurement.

Types of Measurements

There are several methods of measurement commonly used in marketing research and database marketing surveys. These measures are very useful in coding questionnaire responses so that those responses can be entered as numbers into a computer spreadsheet or statistical program for analysis:

Nominal Measures: Nominal measures designate *identity* only. No magnitudes are measured. For example, one nominal measurement might be males = 1, females = 2. Here, 2 is not more than 1; the number 1 simply stands for "male." Nominal data is often used to *code* various respondent characteristics.

Ordinal Measures: Ordinal measures are used to represent differences in magnitude but not degree of magnitude. For example, we might construct a 5-point scale of responses ranging from very low = 1 to very high = 5. In this scale, 2 is more than 1, 3 is more than 2, and so on. But 2 is not twice as much as 1, and 4 is not twice as much as 2. We can only observe that each higher number is greater than the previous number, but we can't say by how much. Ordinal measurements are often used to measure respondent attitudes or opinions with *measurement scales.*

Interval Measures: Interval measurements tell us how far apart the objects or concepts are, but there is no absolute zero point on the scale. The Fahrenheit temperature system is an example of an interval scale. In the case of a thermometer, we can say that the difference between 100 and 120 degrees is the same amount as between 50 and 70 degrees. We cannot say that 100 degrees is twice as hot as 50 degrees, however.

Ratio Measures: Ratio measures are like interval measures except that they possess a meaningful zero point. If we were to want to measure customer height, for example, we could use a ratio scale starting at zero and ranging upward in meters, centimeters, and millimeters. A person's age is also a ratio measure.

The differences between these measurement types are important for several reasons. First, there is more information retained in ratio measures than in interval, ordinal, or nominal measures. There is more information retained in interval data than in ordinal or nominal data. And there is more information retained in ordinal data than in nominal data.

Secondly, the more powerful statistical procedures require interval or ratio data to be valid. There are less powerful methods available for nominal and ordinal data.

Measuring Advertising or Brand Awareness

Advertisers are often interested in knowing whether a population in a target market is aware of their advertising. An auto retailer might run a television ad for a week in his market and then conduct a random survey of households to determine if people are seeing it.

One approach for measuring that awareness might be to conduct a random survey of households and ask respondents to volunteer any recollection of television advertising of automobiles during the last week. This inquiry measures *unprompted* recollections and is assumed to identify those advertisements that made the greatest impression upon respondents (Figure 11.3). Any recollected product advertising is recorded and tabulated after the survey is completed.

A second question might involve *prompting* respondents for all the advertising of specific automobile brands they might have seen on TV during the week. For these questions, the surveyor supplies

> Please list for me all the automobiles you can remember seeing
> advertised on local television programs during the past week.

FIGURE 11.3 Advertising Awareness Survey Question (Unprompted)

a list of automobile brands and asks respondents if they had seen an advertisement for each during the previous week (Figure 11.4). This procedure may serve to remind respondents of advertisements they did see but did not at first recollect. Care must be taken to avoid recollections of ads that did not occur during the period but that might have occurred frequently in the past.

Measuring Attitudes Using Scales

Attitude Surveys Attitudes are of great interest in marketing research because of the belief that attitudes are closely related to behavior. Measurements on attitudes are believed to predict purchasing behavior.

Attitudes may be measured through observation of consumer behavior or through various self-reporting techniques. However, self-reporting is the most widely used method and will be the focus of discussion here.

Self-reported attitudes are typically measured using various *scales*, which are a useful way to assign numbers to concepts so that they are quantified. The quantification assists in conducting analysis by adding machine or computer. With these numbers, we can count different responses, prepare frequency tabulations of multichotomous questions, and calculate percentages.

Attitude scales, however, are seldom constructed to possess the characteristics of ratio or interval measurements. The measurements we get from them have less exactness than measurements on such concepts as weight, height, or age. Most scales tend to use

---

Please tell me whether you have seen commercials on local
television stations since last Sunday for any of the following
automobiles:

☐ Chevrolet
☐ Ford
☐ Toyota   (Check all that are mentioned.)
☐ Honda
☐ Chrysler

Are you sure that you saw these cars advertised during the past
week rather than before last Sunday?

☐ Yes
☐ No

**FIGURE 11.4   Prompting Respondents for Advertisement
Awareness**

nominal or *ordinal* methods of measurement, and this fact has important implications for statistical estimation and testing procedures that can be executed on them to evaluate the riskiness of
accepting survey results as meaningful. In this book, we do not go
into those considerations, but they should be studied by readers
interested in statistical testing and levels of confidence.

Constructing Scales   Scales have a given number of *points*
that are assigned a set of arbitrary numbers. A scale is said to be
balanced if it has an even number of potential responses; an *unbalanced* scale has an uneven number. Balanced scales have no central
value. For some scales, the existence of a central value will have a
special meaning, and unbalanced scales should be used in these
instances. For other purposes, scales will simply indicate an ascending or descending series of values, and for these cases, balanced scales are perfectly appropriate.

The points along a scale have *ordinal* relationships. For example, a 5-point scale might have points assigned the numbers 1, 2, 3, 4, and 5, indicating an ascending order of magnitude. Point 2 would be greater than point 1, and so forth. The lower end, described by the number 1, is the lowest value that could be chosen by a respondent. The higher end, described by the number 5, is the highest value that could be chosen by a respondent.

Scales can be assigned any number of points depending on the measure desired by the researcher, the character of the question asked, and the analytical procedures to be used on the data generated. For example, a 2-point scale might be used for a question requiring low or high responses. A 3-point scale might be used for a question with three potential answers, for example, poor $= 1$, average $= 2$, and good $= 3$.

Five-point scales are frequently used to allow respondents to express intensity of feelings while minimizing variance in the data. Customer satisfaction questionnaires often present 5-point scales like the following: 1 = very dissatisfied, 2 = dissatisfied, 3 = neither satisfied nor dissatisfied, 4 = satisfied, and 5 = very satisfied.

Greater numbers of points on a scale, such as 7, 9, 11, or 13 points, are occasionally selected to build greater variance into the responses. High levels of variance are sometimes useful for special statistical analysis.

Often, researchers will add a point response that is off their scale of potential responses to permit the respondent to answer "I don't know." For example, consider Figure 11.5.

Researchers must be careful to avoid forcing a respondent to answer from a set of fixed alternatives if none of them applies to her. A customer who has no knowledge of a product cannot answer a question asking for feedback about that product. If this happens, the customer may leave the question blank or may answer with a central value such as "neither approve nor disapprove" in Figure 11.5. The researcher may decide that blank responses render the questionnaire invalid. Moreover, "neither approve nor disapprove" is not a correct response either.

Question	Strongly disapprove	Disapprove	Neither disapprove nor approve	Approve	Strongly approve	Don't know
Do you approve or disapprove of Senate Bill 451?	1	2	3	4	5	9

FIGURE 11.5   Providing for "Don't Know" Answers

Types of Scales   There are a variety of types of scales utilized in marketing research today. In this section, several of the more popular scales are described. You should investigate each method thoroughly before attempting to put it to use in your own research study.

1. *Likert Summated Rating Scale.* The Likert scale provides a method for the respondent to express the intensity of feeling about a product or business attribute. Each respondent is asked to indicate the extent of his agreement with a statement. The extent of disagreement or agreement becomes a point along a predefined scale measuring responses (Figure 11.6).

   Any measurement scale should be tested and validated for consistency in measuring the concept it is intended to measure. For example, arbitrarily constructed Likert Scales are subject to a potential problem in consistently discriminating between favorable and unfavorable measurements. If a sample of customers is favorably inclined toward a store, their ratings on a scale constructed to measure their attraction should all be relatively positive. Questions using measurement scales that solicit inconsistently positive and negative responses from individuals who are positively disposed toward a store are not good discriminators of the concept being measured by the scale and should be discarded.

173

Issue	Strongly disagree	Disagree	Neither agree or disagree	Agree	Strongly agree
	1	2	3	4	5
1. The store's service is very good.	☐	☐	☐	☐	☐
2. The store's product quality is very poor.	☐	☐	☐	☐	☐
3. The store's prices are very attractive.	☐	☐	☐	☐	☐

FIGURE 11.6   Likert Scales

Researchers should test all potential statements with a large sample of persons and discard those that are not good discriminators. In practice, many studies are performed on untested statements using the Likert Summated Rating Scale. Likert scales can also be used to calculate a total score by adding the scores for many scales.

2. *Semantic Differential Scale.* The Semantic Differential Scale is constructed by anchoring each end of a multiple-point scale with statements that are semantic opposites of one another. For example, one end of the scale might be labeled "This product is very good," while the other would be labeled "This product is very poor." The midpoint of the scale, then, would be neither good nor bad and would show a feeling of ambivalence about the product.

Semantic differential scales are very popular in the marketing literature because of their ease of construction. With these scales, respondents can express the intensity of their feelings toward a company, a product, packaging, advertising, or virtually any other feature in the marketing effort. However, like the Likert Scales, they should be tested for consistency in discriminating favorable from unfavorable responses through a purifying procedure.

A sample of several semantic differential scales using a 5-point scale are displayed in Figure 11.7.

The semantic differential scale is especially useful for comparing two businesses. For example, the respondent could be presented with sets of identical scales—one set for your own business and another set for a competitor. In this way, each question would be answered for your business and again for the competitor, and you could use the responses to get feedback on how customers are comparing your own business with your competitor.

On a survey form, the orientation of the scales is generally jumbled to prevent respondents from answering without examining each issue. In jumbled format, negative poles of scales are sometimes positioned at the left end and sometimes at the right.

3. *Rating Scales.* Yet another scaling technique in common use, rating scales are used to assess the importance of a product feature in decision making. In Figure 11.8, a rating scale is used

Lower pole	1	2	3	4	5	Upper pole
1. Restaurant is extremely messy and dirty.	☐	☐	☐	☐	☐	Restaurant is extremely neat and clean.
2. Service is very slow.	☐	☐	☐	☐	☐	Service is very quick.
3. Hours are very inconvenient.	☐	☐	☐	☐	☐	Hours are very convenient.

FIGURE 11.7 Semantic Differential Scale

Please evaluate each of the following attributes for its importance for you by checking the appropriate boxes.

Attribute	Not important	Somewhat important	Fairly important	Very important
1. The store's service is very good.	☐	☐	☐	☐
2. The store's product quality is very good.	☐	☐	☐	☐
3. The store's prices are very attractive.	☐	☐	☐	☐

FIGURE 11.8 Using a Rating Scale for Importance Measures

to illustrate how importance indicators for each product or store feature question might be rated.

For each statement in this example, "Not important" marks the lowest point on this scale, whereas "Very important" marks the highest point. There are four points on this balanced scale, and they might be coded as 1, 2, 3, and 4, respectively, from lowest to highest importance.

GOOD SURVEY PRACTICES

Over the years, experience has taught marketing research professionals which practices tend to produce a good survey result. You would do well to follow these suggestions:

- Send a letter ahead of the survey mailing/calls announcing and explaining the upcoming survey.
- Use your marketing database to personalize cover letters and questionnaires. Modern word processors almost always have a

merge feature that allows you to insert phrases, names, dates, and other information into the salutation and body of documents.

- Explain the objective of a mail survey in your cover letter and in the survey form itself.
- Assure the customer or prospect in both cover letter and survey that the information provided will be kept confidential.
- When you are designing a survey, *always* test every question on a small sample of customers or prospects like those to be surveyed. No matter how clearly worded the survey form seems to you, your respondents will always recognize some other interpretation than the one you intended.
- Adding the phrase "No salesperson will call" to the survey form's introduction generally helps the response, but make sure it is true if you include it. Database marketers, for example, fully intend to contact the respondent soon after receipt of the survey form.
- Include a brief explanation of why your survey is important to the respondent in both the cover letter and survey form.
- Explain to each survey recipient why he in particular is being surveyed. If his name was drawn as a result of a random sample, tell him that. If every customer is being surveyed, tell him that.
- Offer an incentive for the customer's cooperation: A gift such as a dollar bill or a discount coupon the next time the customer is in the store.
- Instruct the respondent where to send the completed survey (if it's a mail survey). Be sure to include a self-addressed and stamped envelope for the return.
- Instruct each survey respondent of the deadline for sending the completed survey form back (if it's a mail survey). A deadline will encourage the return. If it is not returned, follow up with a second mailing for those who have not returned their forms.
- If the mail survey is to be sent to organizations, offer to share a summary of survey results with the respondent.

- If you already have some items of information about each customer or prospect being surveyed, do not ask for them in your survey.
- Keep your mail survey questionnaire as brief as possible. One page is better than two. Two pages are much better than three. Response rates drop as survey length rises.
- Conduct follow-up telephone calls to non-respondents. Offer to take their responses over the telephone.

DISGUISED VERSUS UNDISGUISED SURVEYS

If you are using the survey as a dialogue-building device, you must identify who the sponsor of the survey is. But in some cases, knowledge of who the sponsor is can cause the respondent to modify an answer. To the database marketer, developing a friendly and honest relationship is more important in this case than the accuracy of the data. To the database marketer, the personal response to every single communication of a customer or prospect is important in retaining customers and gaining new ones. Therefore, surveys from such a marketer will invariably contain a request for the respondent's name and address. This request may influence what the respondent is willing to indicate in her responses.

If you require an unbiased survey, you may want to administer the survey without identifying the sponsor. An unidentified survey is called a *disguised survey*. Maintaining anonymity is one reason many businesses hire a third-party research firm to administer their surveys. Market researchers have known for years, for example, that knowledge of the sponsor of a survey can distort the answers given by respondents. To make a point or just to express irritation with the survey, complaints may be overstated, motivations may be concealed, or comparisons with competitors may be biased. Offering the respondent the opportunity to remain unidentified also helps to get to her genuine feelings and opinions. To the database marketer, an anonymous survey is a useless survey. If it cannot be tied back to specific customers in his database, it cannot be responded to and cannot be used to build a relationship with the respondent.

CHOOSING BETWEEN A MAIL OR TELEPHONE SURVEY

Years ago, surveys were occasionally performed door to door by personal interviewers. In some areas, the national decennial census is still done that way. However, as women have gradually moved from the home to the workplace, it has become very difficult to find sampled household adults at home during daylight hours. And as the security of many neighborhoods has deteriorated, it has become harder to find interviewers willing to go into certain neighborhoods. As a result, the expense and low completion rates of door-to-door surveying has increased the costs of these types of surveys. Administration of surveys by telephone and mail has subsequently increased in popularity.

Telephone Interviewing

Surveying by telephone has certain advantages and disadvantages. Telephone interviewing allows greater complexity in the questionnaire than does mail surveying, but mail permits the inclusion of product illustrations, diagrams, and photographs. Here are some other advantages associated with telephone interviewing by professional research firms:[1]

- Telephone sampling enables researchers to select and interview large, geographically dispersed samples of respondents.
- Telephone interviewing by professional marketing research firms is conducted in a centralized facility with professional supervisors. Training of interviewers can be standardized, and

supervision can ensure consistent administration of question-naires.

- Telephone interviews can be efficiently conducted for very large numbers of respondents, so a study can be completed in a relatively short period of time.
- Pretesting a survey questionnaire can be completed in very short order.
- Callbacks can be made easily when a scheduled call finds no one at home.

Several disadvantages associated with telephone interviewing, however, are as follows:

- It is very hard to maintain a telephone interview beyond 10 to 15 minutes. Respondents begin to feel imposed on.
- Certain types of measurement techniques are difficult to use in telephone interviews. Lengthy scales are hard for some respondents to understand. Card-sorting techniques are impossible to administer.
- The interviewer is not able to use pictures, exhibits, or drawings to illustrate a product or situation.

The entrepreneur or business manager who tries to do his own telephone interview may not realize all these advantages or disadvantages, however. Whereas a professional research firm might desire to use a 7-point attitude scale to measure a response, the novice may be quite content with a high-low answer. However, a manager might combine mail and telephone surveys by mailing drawings and brochures and then following up by telephone for an interview.

If the market area for a business lies within a limited radius around the business location, geographic dispersion of survey respondents may not be a critical factor. Small-town residents might enjoy a lengthy interview with a local businessperson. City residents, however, would probably resent the interruption during their evening relaxation after work.

The purpose of a survey, after all, is to gain an understanding of the customer's viewpoint. That can be achieved with a little honest dialogue in many cases without full use of all the tools of the market researchers' trade. Sometimes, complex designs and measurements are necessary because professionals tend to be impersonal, brisk, assertive, and hurried in their administration of a survey. Small businesspeople telephoning local residents or businesses can take more time, be more friendly, and be less structured in their questioning, and this can make an important difference.

Mail Surveys

For the entrepreneur or small business manager, mail surveys are very attractive because they are easy to do. They are relatively inexpensive to send out.[2] Ofttimes, the sample sizes can be very large without significantly increasing the survey costs owing to cost savings in printing. Mail surveys can reach households and businesses wherever they may be geographically; there is no need to worry about unlisted telephone numbers. Exhibits, illustrative pictures, and drawings of products can be included right on the questionnaire to support survey questions. And because no interviewer is involved, there can be no biasing because of interviewer inexperience or distracting comments.

On the other hand, mail surveys often have very low rates of return—sometimes as low as 10 percent. In those instances, it's suspected that those who do return mail surveys may be answering questions in ways that are not representative of the total population receiving the surveys. The conclusions one reaches from such data, therefore, might be wrong and lead to ineffective decisions by management.

Although the designer of a mail survey can insert screening questions and instructions for directing the survey to the desired respondents, there is little control over who completes the survey.

When a question is not understood by the respondent, he may not complete it in the way intended, if at all. (Sometimes this problem can be handled by including a toll-free telephone number on the survey form for respondents to call should they have questions or problems with the survey.)

To have a chance of getting a good rate of return, you generally must have a specific name to whom to send the questionnaire. Mailing to "Occupant" simply won't do. Thus, you must either have an in-house mailing list or be able to purchase a suitable sample (hopefully random) from a list broker—a specialist in compiling mailing and telephone lists for use in marketing programs and reseach studies.

Finally, the speed with which mail surveys are completed is controlled by the rate at which respondents get around to completing them and mailing them back. On the other hand, a mail survey can be designed, implemented, and analyzed by one person with a fair degree of autonomy and economy. It is difficult for a single person to design, manage, implement, and analyze a telephone survey.

SUMMARY

With a little effort, the entrepreneur or business manager can design and launch her own surveying project. The initial efforts may be relatively unproductive due to low returns, biased samples, omitted questions, or poor measurements, but she will learn from these experiences and do better with practice.

If you would like to try your own survey, don't forget to *test your questionnaire* on a small sample of those people you expect to complete it. If a survey is worth doing, it will be worth the time and effort to make sure your survey form is a good one.

INTERVIEWING

12

Data collection by mail or telephone surveys are only two options open to the marketing researcher. Individuals may be given *personal interviews* or invited to participate in interactive meetings called *focus groups*.

SURVEYS VERSUS INTERVIEWS

In practice, interviewing generally complements surveys administered by mail or telephone. Although not all surveys are highly structured in their format, most tend to contain more structured questions and fixed-response answers than open-ended queries. In mail surveys, usually no other interaction occurs between the questioner and the respondent than what is written on the questionnaire. Even in telephone surveys, surveyors tend to minimize conversation or discussion other than the exact wording on the questionnaire. This standardization of the questions is an attempt to minimize differences in interpretation by ensuring that each respondent hears exactly the same question in exactly the same way.

The problem with structured surveys, of course, is that they only capture snapshots, as it were, of people's decision-making processes. Moreover, those snapshots are taken from the perspective of the designer of the survey questionnaire. Only those inquiries designed into the questionnaire appear in the portrait taken.

Attitude questions, for example, request information about respondents' feelings, not about their actual behavior. Questions that ask about purchasing intentions discover only that: intentions. Follow-ups to those surveyed will find that many do not do as they reported they were inclined to do.

Structured surveys don't, and probably can't, capture a full understanding of a complex decision-making or purchasing process or anticipate fully the assumptions or motivations behind it. They invariably omit questions about influencing factors. Designers of questionnaires simplify the decision-making process based on the factors they anticipate or understand to be most important.

Economic and marketing models generally guide the survey designers to include the major factors in their questionnaires: price, service, product quality, distribution, and promotion. But within each of those factors lies a large number of emotion-charged issues that pertain not to economics but to personal preference, relationships, choices of lifestyle, life-stage, feelings, fears and insecurities, the need to be liked and respected, and so forth.

The creative task of an advertising agency, for example, is to harness those associations so that a product has an emotional appeal to customers. Marketers use their knowledge of customer motivations and preferences to position their product as a luxury car, a quality television, an affordable dress, a dependable washing machine, and the like. So it is often the understanding that marketers gain of the motivations and self-images of their customers that determines much of their success in the marketplace.

Much of that understanding emerges from face-to-face meetings and dialogue with actual and potential customers. For this reason, the business manager would be wise to consider using personal interviews and focus groups as tools to enhance her understanding of customers and prospects (Figure 12.1).

PERSONAL INTERVIEWS

The personal interview is probably the most widely used method for collecting information in the business world today. Every day, people in business and government encounter problems about which they know little. To educate themselves, they identify experts within or outside their organization. Then they contact those experts, probably by telephone. They explain their problem and

FIGURE 12.1   Conducting an Interview

ask for advice, insights, references, or information on potential solutions. Ofttimes this exploratory research leads to networking
from person to person until the requester feels that he has sufficient
information to make a judgment about likely solutions.

There are, however, clear advantages to conducting even structured interviews in person. Here are several:

- With telephone or mail surveys, the selection of respondents is
  guided by available telephone listings and mailing lists. With
  personal interviews, you can control who you interview.[1]
- The personal interview provides the greatest degree of control
  to the researcher. If you wish for your questionnaire to be answered only by male heads-of-household, you can make sure
  that those are the only persons from whom data is collected.
  Moreover, nonresponse owing to refusals is lower than for either mail or telephone surveys.
- A personal interview is one of the most effective ways to capture in-depth attitude or opinion information.[2]
- The interviewer has the greatest flexibility in survey length and
  structure.
- You can remove the interviewee from a social situation in which
  she might be influenced in her answers. A potential problem,
  however, is that the respondent may react to the interviewer's
  presence as well.
- In a personal interview, the interviewer can see the behavior of
  the respondent. He can observe body language, facial expres-
  sion, and discomfort or animation and hear emotion in the
  voice of the respondent. This provides an opportunity to probe
  and gain a greater understanding of the motivations, feelings,
  and thought processes behind attitudes, expressed intentions,
  and answers to interviewer questions.
- The interviewer can present exhibits, pictures, advertisements,
  and other displays to the respondent for testing or reactions.

A large number of structured and unstructured questions answered during face-to-face interviews can provide a more compre-

hensive and informative database for analyzing and solving marketing problems than the mail or telephone responses from a simple structured questionnaire.

However, finding the intended respondents at home is often very difficult, and in many instances the interviewing must be scheduled for evenings or weekends. Also, interviewers must travel extensively to reach respondents in random samples, and with missed appointments, researchers can experience serious problems with high staffing and travel costs as well as slow progress on data collection.[3]

Unfortunately, face-to-face interviewing is also the most expensive data collection method. It is expensive in terms of the time it takes to complete a series of interviews, and it is expensive in terms of dollar outlays for travel, interviewer salaries, and compensation of respondents for their time and trouble.

FOCUS GROUPS

In a focus group interview, a small number of individuals meets together for a collective interview with an interviewer (Figure 12.2). The number of panelists generally numbers between 8 and 12 individuals, although occasionally groups of 5 or 6 panelists are assembled. The setting is typically around an oval or rectangular table in an isolated room.

Focus groups conducted by professional marketing research firms often utilize a specially designed room that permits clients to view the focus group through a one-way mirror. Verbatim tape recordings and even videotapes of the sessions can be arranged as well with research companies.

When to Use Focus Groups

Focus groups have been successful in many different situations. The following are some suggestions on when to use this method:

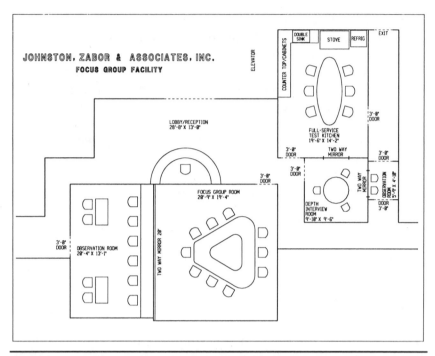

FIGURE 12.2 Design of a Focus Group and Interviewing Facility

- Use a focus group as an exploratory technique when no one has a clear idea of how customers or prospects are viewing a product or what the problem might be.
- Use a focus group as an information-gathering technique to learn enough about customer situations and concerns so that a structured questionnaire can be constructed.
- Use a focus group to test whether the wording of a questionnaire is understood as intended by potential respondents.
- Use a focus group as part of an orientation to help new marketing or sales personnel gain greater insights into how prospective customers think, feel, and talk about their products.
- Use a focus group for gathering insights into how potential customers might react to a new product or service.

- Use a focus group to pretest advertising concepts or the creative focus of product ads.
- Use a focus group to assess how a corporate acquisition might influence the trust that current customers have in products or services.[4]

Those professionals who plan and conduct focus groups know that there are few hard and fast rules on how or when to use them in a research effort. However, focus groups are most helpful when used to help understand a marketing problem or customer segment. They are not substitutes for a carefully designed random survey of the market, and neither are they generally used for relationship building.

The Limitations of Focus Groups as a Research Method

Although useful in many instances as an exploratory device, an early component of a survey research project, or in conducting in-depth investigations into customer motivation, the focus group is not without its limitations. Here are a few of the problems:

- The panelists on a focus group are neither numerous nor selected at random, so the dialogue and the conclusions of the group cannot be projected with any confidence to the greater population.
- Focus groups are a relatively inexpensive method of conducting research and are sometimes performed by a business as a substitute for more scientifically designed surveys.
- The examination of marketing issues presented to focus group panelists does not occur in the real world. Decisions in daily life are made in a constantly changing environment.
- Focus groups are sometimes used for purposes other than gaining insights into the motivations, feelings, and reactions of people. For example, some entrepreneurs have done focus groups,

edited the videotapes, and then used those tapes as a marketing device to seek financial support from banks and venture capitalists.[5]

PLANNING A FOCUS GROUP

If you are thinking about conducting your own focus group, the following suggestions might be helpful.

1. *Planning*

   - Define carefully just what you need to achieve from the focus group.

   - Is the research problem appropriate for a focus group? Is it a problem calling for a quantitative survey and a larger, random sample?

   - What exhibits, products, or materials will you need to show the panelists? Are those materials available for the focus group?

   - Prepare a *discussion guide* (or annotated agenda) detailing the discussion areas to be covered, the tasks to be assigned to panelists during the session, and the scenarios that will be constructed during the session.

   - Prepare a *screener* to aid in the recruiting of appropriate panelists. The screener is a short questionnaire that can be used to identify potential panelists for your focus group. If you felt, for example, that the right candidates for your focus group were retired senior women who had careers in the arts, you would construct several questions for your screener about age, sex, current workforce status, and past employment.

   - Estimate the costs for your focus group. Table 12.1 will serve as a worksheet for estimating your costs.

TABLE 12.1   Focus Group Planning Worksheet

Component	Planning notes	Cost
Staffing		
Planning		
Recruitment of focus group participants		
Focus group facilitator		
Staff travel		
Equipment and supplies	Microphones and sound system. Flip charts, magic markers, note pads, pens. Videotaping equipment.	
Meeting facilities		
Room	A room designed specifically to serve as a focus group facility will cost $350–$500 per event.	
Refreshments	Refreshments for both participants and observers, if any.	
Audio recording	If the room has a sound system, cost is additional.	
Video	If the room is designed to permit videotaping from a hidden location, cost is additional.	
Transcription		
Written report with analysis		
Participants		
Stipends	Stipend to focus groups participants varies from approximately $40 each for consumer goods to $100 plus for business decision makers.	
Expenses	It is customary to cover the cost of travel for focus group participants to and from the meeting.	
Subtotal		
Other overhead expenses	Apportioned shares of business telephone costs, utilities, postage, copying, computers and word processing, marketing literature, etc.	
Total		

2. *Scheduling Focus Group Interviews* How many focus groups should you do, and where should they be held? Large cities are convenient, but panelists will probably share a local cultural bent. You could do focus groups in several cities to assess the effect of location, of course. Small town or rural locations will be less costly in terms of facility rental and panelist compensation. Depending upon the locations of your recruited panelists, travel costs (which you should pay for) may be a significant consideration.

3. *The focus group session* Selection of the environment of the focus group session is a decision of some importance. Too comfortable a setting, for example, may be inappropriate to support the intensity generated within many of these sessions. As a result, some moderators prefer a relatively formal setting. You will also want to consider the advantages of recording or even videotaping the session.

4. *The debriefing* The debriefing is the recap among members of the focus group staff team immediately following the session. The team discusses the dynamics of the session, which techniques worked well and which did not work as hoped, and what each team member learned during the session.

Selecting Panelists

The task of selecting panelists for your focus group flows directly from several basic planning questions:

- What is the purpose of this project?
- How many people need to be interviewed?
- What composition of panelists should be selected to best fulfill the purpose of the project?
- How many of the recruited panelists are likely to appear at the appointed hour for the focus group?
- What compensation should be offered to panelists?

Project Purpose   A focus group to get insights into the factors going into corporate decision making by chief executive officers (CEOs) will require panelists who are CEOs. A focus group to gather information about homemakers' uses of detergents will require panelists who are homemakers.

Size of Focus Group   A significant number of professional focus group facilitators argue that focus groups of 4 to 6 panelists are optimum. However, most facilitators probably prefer groups from 8 to 12 persons. Some of the issues that may bear on the size of the group selected include

- Will the size of group affect the opportunities for any given panelist to speak?
- Will the size of the group affect the depth of discussion permitted during a two-hour session?
- Will the size of the group affect the ability of the moderator to control the pace and character of discussions?

Advocates of smaller groups feel that they display higher energy in discussions and are more orderly and controllable.[6] They are also less expensive.

Focus Group Composition   To generate discussion and varying insights, a focus group must contain panelists of differing backgrounds and viewpoints. The recruitment of highly heterogenous panels, however, can be taken to such an extreme that none of the panelists share the views, opinions, or perspectives of the others. In such cases, conversation will stall, and panelists may be unable or unwilling to communicate their feelings. On the other hand, if a panel is recruited which is too homogeneous in its views, the discussions may be very limited in terms of the insights gained.

Overrecruiting   Experienced focus group moderators know that all of the recruited panelists seldom show up at the appointed time for the meeting. Some forget the session. Others have an emergency and cannot come. Others simply change their mind about participating.

To compensate for these no-shows, recruiters overrecruit for focus groups. The extent of overrecruiting varies but is often in the range of 20 percent. For a final panel of 10 persons, recruiters will recruit perhaps 12 persons.

Compensation   Compensation for participating in a focus group will vary from region to region and even between urban and rural areas. Payments of from $25 to $50 for each panelist for a two-hour session are probably common today for projects focused at consumers. However, to attract business decision makers to focus groups, payments might range from $75 to $250 each for a two-hour session.

The Focus Group Team

Various staffing arrangements for conducting a focus group are in use. I myself prefer a three-person team comprised of a *moderator*, a *reporter*, and a *resource person*. The moderator is at once a participant and a leader of the group. He manages the dynamics of the group, guides the panelists to reveal themselves and their motivations, and ensures that the session stays on schedule as it works through the discussion plan.

The *reporter* captures the main points of the discussion on a flip chart and, if possible, tapes the completed pages on the focus group room walls so that panelists can have them available for reference. The reporter also supports the moderator by watching panelists for emerging problems, body language, and signs of confusion or non-participation.

The *resource person* is an expert on the details or technical facets of the issues under discussion and can be called upon for information when needed. She is generally passive in the session and does not volunteer information or take part in the dialogue but responds to requests for information by the moderator or panelists.

However, many professional focus group facilitators prefer to conduct focus groups alone or with only a recorder. Doing a group solo can help reduce your costs, too.

Running a Focus Group

As a member of the focus group team, whether of several persons or of one only, you need to execute your role within the session in a way that helps panelists to accomplish the purposes set for the meeting:

- Relax the participants and develop a trusting and open atmosphere in which dialogue can occur spontaneously.
- Start off the session by explaining the way the group will operate, what your role will be, who the client is (if the session will be undisguised), and what the objectives of the focus group will be.
- Conduct introductions for yourself and the panelists in a way that will relax the panelists and help them to enjoy their participation. The introductions are a good time for games and a little silliness to get people laughing and feeling good.
- Show the panelists your unannotated agenda and follow it throughout the session.
- Avoid asking direct questions that can be answered with a word or two. The moderator's goal is to help the panelists reveal their own motivations, feelings, and reasoning. Instead of direct questioning, use promptings such as

    How do you react to this product/advertising concept?

    Tell us what you mean by that.

    Offer the group a positive feature and a negative feature about this advertisement.

Why do you feel that way?

What would be a better way to communicate this concept?

- Monitor each topic listed in your discussion guide to make sure that you achieve your goals before going on to the next topic.
- Work to become accepted by panelists as a trusted member of the group and as its procedural leader.
- Consistently turn issues or questions addressed to you or your team members back to the group for discussion or analysis. Avoid leading the group or taking on the role of an expert.
- Protect vulnerable panelists from criticism and use the group to control overly aggressive panelists.
- Always show respect to each member of the panel. Help them to reveal their feelings and meanings through displaying genuine curiosity about their points of view.

If you are interested in learning more about how to do your own focus groups, consider the following two books for a more comprehensive treatment than I could provide here:

- Richard A. Krueger, *Focus Groups: A Practical Guide for Applied Research* (Thousand Oaks, CA: Sage Publications, 1994).
- Jane Farley Templeton, *Focus Group: A Guide for Marketing or Advertising Professionals* (Chicago: Probus Publishing, 1987).

Personal interviews, focus groups, and surveys represent the principal tools used by marketing researchers to gather primary data. They are frequently used in solving marketing problems that appear unexpectedly during the implementation of the marketing plan. We now turn to discussing how marketing researchers approach problem-solving projects.

PROBLEM SOLVING WITH MARKETING RESEARCH

13

Marketing research can be used to solve marketing problems, just as it can be used to develop stronger marketing plans or to create systems for monitoring the marketplace. In fact, problem solving is probably the most common use of marketing research methodology. Some of the types of problems you can solve using marketing research methods include

1. *Product problems*

   - Company sales or sales of a product line have taken an unexpected downward turn. You are uncertain of the cause of the downturn and need to diagnose the causes so you can correct the trend.

   - You are planning on introducing a new product, but are unsure how the market will respond to the introduction. You need to know

     The best combination of new product features to include

How to price it

Where (geographically) to introduce it

- An important competitor introduces a new product. You need to know how to respond to that introduction.

2. *Pricing problems*

- A competitor has reduced its price for a competing product. Should you follow suit or pursue some other course?

- When you reduce your price, total revenues increase. Why is that? And how far should you reduce your price before profits start to decline?

3. *Distribution problems*

- Where should you store your inventories and in what quantities?

- Your products are not moving well through independent agents and brokers. Should you increase the commissions to agents and brokers to improve the sales of your products or would some other action be better for you?

4. *Promotional problems*

- What product benefits are the most important for advertising themes? Which creative approaches will work best with your customers?

- What sales incentives would work best for your business? And specifically what minimum incentives should you consider?

For the small businessperson, however, using the problem-solving methods of marketing research presents some significant challenges. Because each problem represents something of a special situation, each study must be designed from scratch. And although there are a number of fairly standard tools for analysis, one has to decide in which cases to use which tools and how exactly to use them. Moreover, some of those tools are very challenging theoretically as well as mathematically.

This single chapter cannot provide adequate instructions to prepare the typical businessperson to overcome all those requirements. What it can do is present the logic of the problem-solving process, do a little case study, review some basic ways of summarizing data, and conduct some elementary analysis. That logic—essentially the scientific method—can be discussed.

DEFINING THE PROBLEM

One of the major tasks for those who do marketing research is designing research that correctly identifies the causes of marketing problems. This research is generally dictated by a decision maker who decides that she has a marketing problem of some kind. The problem may have its roots in the environment or in the policies of the firm. In problem-solving marketing research, creating a research design that will solve the decision maker's dilemma is step one.

A CASE STUDY

Suppose you were the president of a farm and garden supply business named Max's Farm Supply. You have noticed a problem with declining sales in one of your biggest sellers—a very profitable line of pesticide products. Your sales director has almost convinced you that the problem is that prices in this product line have been set too high, but you are not quite ready to believe him. You suspect that the problem is that your sales force has not been trying hard enough to sell these products.

The sales director has been urging you to advertise these products, but you have no faith in advertising to solve the problem. In fact, you feel that advertising is a waste of money. You are also very proud of your company's reputation for long-standing integrity and of its many loyal customers.

Because of your uncertainty over whether to blame the declines in sales on pricing or on the sales force, you request that a marketing research study be assigned to one of the sales director's staff members. The research analyst, whose name is Robin, is assigned the work without being allowed to discuss the problem with you, but she is urged by the sales director to document the disparity in product prices with the competition, which, he believes, accounts for the declines in sales. Robin does not know, for example, that you suspect a problem with sales, and neither does she know what other causes you might suspect or what actions you might entertain.

There are only three retailers in the city selling these products: Lowe's, Lawn & Garden, and Max's Farm Supply.

SETTING UP THE RESEARCH PROJECT

Robin does her homework on her assignment. She is very frustrated with her lack of information on your views about the project or on what actions you would be willing to take should she identify the causes of the sales decline. However, given the character of your store and the very hierarchical style of management in your business, she suspects that you will probably not entertain radical changes in how you do business.

First, she checks a research textbook to clarify how to plan her project. The textbook suggests ordering her planning into six steps or stages:

- Formulating the decision and research problem
- Creating the research design
- Deciding how data is to be collected, and designing questionnaires, if any
- Designing the sample and data collection methods

- Analyzing and interpreting the data
- Reporting on the results[1]

Formulating the Decision and Research Problems

Robin understands that you expect her to present alternatives on how to at least restore the pesticide product category to its previous level of sales.

Hence, she defines the decision problem:

> Identify what management might do to restore sales of pesticide products.

She then asks what information is required to help solve this decision problem, and how to get that information for the study—in other words, what is the research problem?

> Determine which company policies or environmental causes were responsible for the sales decline.

Creating the Research Design

Solving the research problem, however, depends on which of several possible causes might lie behind the decline in sales for this product line. Therefore, she decides to first do some initial exploratory research on possible causes by interviewing the salespeople, a marketing professor at a local university, and an executive friend who works at a local advertising agency. As a result of her exploratory research, she decides that seven alternative factors could feasibly lie behind the decline in sales:

- Pricing disparities with Max's competition
- Max's current products are meeting fewer customers' needs for some reason.
- Competitors have introduced lines of pesticides that are meeting customer needs better.
- Poor performance by Max's sales staff.
- Service problems with these products.
- Falling product awareness by the potential buyers of these products due to competitor promotions of their products.
- Environmental factors.

This seems a long list to Robin, but she is unable to reduce the possible number of feasible causes. Each of them seems to imply a different set of courses of action to correct the problem. She decides that she will be able to do an exploratory and a descriptive analysis by

- Observing the behaviors of competitors
- Surveying the attitudes and perceptions of a random sample of pesticide customers and prospects of the three stores
- Doing an experience survey through visits, telephone interviews, and letter writing to officials who are experts about pesticides and the pesticide industry
- Examining internal records on sales personnel performance

To keep herself organized, Robin prepares the worksheet displayed in Table 13.1. In her worksheet, she sets forth her plan for gathering the information she requires, including the information needed and how she expects to collect it. She also thinks through how she intends to analyze the information she will gather.

Data Collection Methods and Questionnaires

Pricing Data and New Product Introductions   Robin has determined that she should visit both competing stores and doc-

TABLE 13.1 The Research Design

Alternative causes	What information is required?	How to get that data?	How to analyze that data?
1. Price disparities with competitors.	Competitor prices on comparable products. Max's prices on each product.	Visit each competitor's store. Obtain price list for Max's pesticide products.	Compare prices for comparable types and sizes of products.
2. Max's products are not meeting customer needs as well.	Feedback from customers who have purchased these products in the past but who have not purchased them lately.	Survey of past customers.	Analyze reasons for no recent purchases.
3. Competitors have introduced new and improved products.	Any new products that competitors have placed on the market and how well they are doing.	Visits to competitor stores. Survey past customers of Max's as well as customers of Max's competitors.	Determine whether buyers are switching over to any new products.
4. Max's salespeople are falling off in their productivity.	Sales data of each salesperson by product line.	Computer printout of internal sales records of each salesperson *by product line* over the past two years.	Check to see if any salespeople have dropped in sales for this product line alone. If so, find out why.

Continued on next page

TABLE 13.1 *(continued)*

Alternative causes	What information is required?	How to get that data?	How to analyze that data?
5. Service problems with these products.	Customer feedback on service received when purchasing these products in the past.	Survey of past customers of Max's.	Identify whether customers feel that they have not been supported with good use and product information when purchasing these products.
6. Fall in Max's customer product awareness by potential buyers.	Have competitors been advertising their products? What have potential buyers done as a result of that advertising?	Survey of buyers to identify awareness of ads. Clippings of competitor advertisements.	Assess whether competitors' advertisements are inducing Max's customers to try their brands.
7. Environmental factors.	Have there been changes in product use caused by economic, political, or social events?	Contact university agricultural extension service. Write letter to Environmental Protection Agency. Call manufacturers of product lines sold by Max's and the two other competitors.	Determine whether consumers are using less pesticide or whether regulatory agencies are modifying past regulations on pesticide use.

ument the brands, prices, and volume discount structures of their competing products. At each store, she notes the brands, sizes, prices of each size, and manufacturer of each. She purchases a small container of each brand before she leaves the store.

Robin also records the shelf space devoted to each brand (the number of "facings" each brand has received on the shelf) because she knows that the shelf volume devoted to a product is determined by each product's turnover and case volume. Faster-turning stock is given more shelf space to avoid having to stock shelves frequently.

She then finds a stockperson to ask for "advice" on selecting the right pesticide for her garden. From the stockpeople, she learns which are the fastest-selling products and which are new brands. She asks about quantity discounts and discovers that, unlike Max's Farm Supply, neither Lowe's nor Lawn & Garden gives quantity discounts on their products.

Advertising by Competitors   Although Robin anticipates that she will need to ask people in her survey about their reactions to advertising by competitors, she also recognizes that she will have to study the advertising strategies of Max's competitors. She quickly finds that both concentrate their advertising in the local newspaper rather than on radio, on television, or in direct mail. Consequently, she begins to build an ad clippings file on both Lowe's and Lawn & Garden.

Both competitors, she finds, tend to bunch their print advertising in local papers on Fridays and Saturdays. She also calls the local advertising manager at the paper and discusses the advertising strategies of the two stores for the past two years. At the first opportunity, she drives to the paper's local offices to visit its newspaper morgue where she spot-checks ads run by the two stores for the past two years.

The ads run by Lawn & Garden appear to be directed toward

women and feature mostly flowers and flowering shrubs in season or light garden and lawn equipment. The ads run by Lowe's are large and utilitarian and cover outdoor tools and mowers, home-building supplies, and hardware. Very rarely are pesticide products advertised, but new products are touted in many ads. For a period of about three months in early 1995, several new pesticide products were prominently featured. Most ad strategies for both stores are based on low prices, wide choices of products, and convenient store locations.

Environmental Events or Trends   After collecting brand samples from each competitor and pulling samples of Max's brands off her own shelves, Robin takes several further steps:

- She calls each of the manufacturers of those products to ask about any sales trends with them and how long each had been on the market.
- She takes the product samples to her university extension service to ask if they are aware of any considerations that might affect the use of any of those brands.
- She writes a letter to the Environmental Protection Agency to ask about any concerns or issues affecting these brands.

From her calls to product manufacturers, she finds that Max's product line is well established and broadly accepted throughout the country. Manufacturers of new products on competitors' shelves, however, report that those new products are being promoted as being less damaging to the environment than Max's brands. This claim is basically endorsed in a return letter from the EPA. Moreover, university extension agents report that the product line on Max's shelves is just beginning to come under criticism by environmental groups. The EPA is said to be preparing new regulations on that product.

Sales Force Productivity   Robin requests a sales performance report from Max's marketing information system manager on each salesperson by month for the pesticide product line for the past two years. Robin also interviews each salesperson about sales in this area. They all report that the big sales were to farmers in the spring and summer months. "We really tried, but farmers did not buy like they did in 1994," salesperson Ann Murray tells her.

"Farmers come in here from 100 miles around," Michael Todd tells Robin. "Last year, 60 percent of our buyers of these products were farmers. We have the best prices in large quantities and make deliveries, but something happened this past year. Farmers just did not come in to buy these products from us. We must have lost our price advantage or something."

The sales report (Table 13.2) provides Robin with the requested data. She quickly establishes that there had been no turnover in salespeople and that the four salespeople working with these products had been loyal employees for years.

From the sales report, she notes that 1994 had been a very good year and that three of the four sales people had exceeded quota. As a result, management had raised each of their quotas for this product line by $5,000. The problem with sales started in the spring of 1995.

In comparing the two years, Robin concludes that Max's sales force probably faced a problem beyond their control. The decline during 1995 is clear in Figure 13.1, where total sales have been graphed by month so that the two years can be compared.

However, the differences among the salespeople's performance against quota—and especially the performance of Todd and Smith—suggest that their work needs a close look. She therefore asks to see their performance evaluations and discusses those records with the sales director.

The performance reviews for Todd and Smith note recent performance problems stemming from personal family difficulties.

TABLE 13.2   Sales Report for Pesticides

Month & Year	Sales dollars				
	Michael Todd	Ann Murray	Tom Ferguson	Sam Smith	Row totals
January 1994	200	250	225	125	800
February 1994	175	200	300	175	850
March 1994	1,475	1,400	1,350	1,250	5,475
April 1994	3,600	5,500	4,400	6,300	19,800
May 1994	10,500	12,050	20,000	11,250	53,800
June 1994	17,500	20,000	22,000	15,000	74,500
July 1994	11,000	10,990	12,500	14,500	48,990
August 1994	6,000	7,500	10,000	10,000	33,500
September 1994	5,000	5,000	7,500	4,000	21,500
October 1994	300	400	300	200	1,200
November 1994	200	225	100	200	725
December 1994	200	100	75	150	525
1994 Subtotals	**56,150**	**63,615**	**78,750**	**63,150**	**261,665**
Annual Sales Quota					
(1994)	**60,000**	**60,000**	**60,000**	**60,000**	**240,000**
Percent of Quota	**94**	**106**	**131**	**105**	**109**
January 1995	125	250	200	124	699
February 1995	100	400	350	200	1,050
March 1995	1,000	990	750	750	3,490
April 1995	1,500	2,000	2,400	4,500	10,400
May 1995	4,500	5,500	13,500	5,500	29,000
June 1995	7,500	9,500	10,525	11,250	38,775
July 1995	6,000	3,000	7,600	7,600	24,200
August 1995	2,200	3,400	4,500	4,400	14,500
September 1995	1,000	1,500	2,300	2,200	7,000
October 1995	350	450	250	250	1,300
November 1995	300	275	300	175	1,050
December 1995	100	125	350	150	725
1995 Subtotals	**24,675**	**27,390**	**43,025**	**37,099**	**132,189**
Annual Sales Quota					
(1995)	**65,000**	**65,000**	**65,000**	**65,000**	**260,000**
Percent of Quota	**38**	**42**	**66**	**57**	**51**

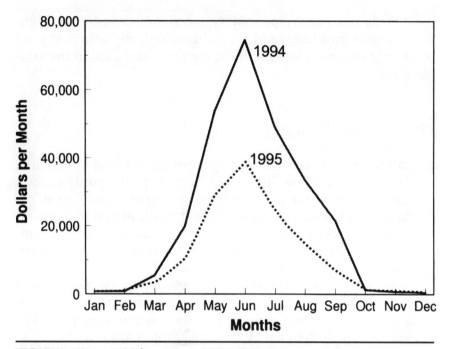

FIGURE 13.1   1994 versus 1995 Sales

Both also needed training, according to their last performance evaluations, in product information.

CONDUCTING A SURVEY

To implement her survey, Robin consults a list broker to help her define and select her sample population. After discussing her needs with the consultant, she decides to select her sample from certain residences and businesses in a six-county area surrounding her store. Her sample will include nurseries, landscaping businesses, farms, and households that can be identified as being "interested in gardening or flowers." She also remembers that units of government in the area have responsibility to maintain the interstate highways, public buildings, and parks; therefore, she asks that local units of government located in the region be included in the sampling frame.

The Sample Design

Robin wants a representative sample from her target population, so she requests that the list broker have its programmer select a random systematic sample from the resulting sampling frame. After discussing her survey plans with a statistician from the university extension service, she decides that she can achieve an acceptable level of accuracy with a sample in the neighborhood of three hundred and fifty respondents.

Robin contracts with this list company for the development of the sample. Sample records will include the name of the owner or head of household, the address, and the telephone number. The systematic sample selected by the broker totals 420 records.

The Questionnaire

Robin goes to work on a questionnaire for her survey of the local pesticide target markets. She designs it to address the following issues:

- Market shares of each store
- Customer satisfaction with products purchased from the three stores
- Customer reasons for their choices among the three stores
- Customer perceptions of service received from each store when purchasing pesticides
- Customer awareness of store advertising
- Store customer profile

The Survey Method

Robin asks for the help of three other office staff at Max's Farm Supply in doing her survey by telephone. The four office workers make the 420 calls over the next three weeks and successfully complete 383 interviews of the sampled households, businesses, and government offices. The remainder of the sample are refusals, not reached or not at the listed address any longer.

Measuring Market Share

Following her survey's introduction and screening questions, Robin includes a question to identify which of the three stores each respondent perceives as his primary source of farm and garden supplies. To obtain this information, Robin includes the question shown in Figure 13.2.

When she tabulates the responses for this question, the result is as follows: Lowe's, 237; Lawn & Garden, 58; Max's Farm Supply, 88. Because these responses are from a random sample of her target market, she calculates that

- Lowe's held a 62 percent market share
- Lawn & Garden held a 15 percent market share
- Max's Farm Supply held a 23 percent market share

Can you tell me from which store in the area you usually buy pesticides and insect control products? *Check the unprompted answer. If respondent cannot remember, name the three stores below for them.*

☐ Lowe's
☐ Lawn & Garden
☐ Max's Farm Supply

FIGURE 13.2 Estimating Market Share

She discusses this result with the sales director and is told that he will find her estimates of market share more useful if they are expressed in terms of sales dollars. He thinks Max's customers spend more on pesticide products on the average than do the customers for either Lowe's or Lawn & Garden.

Robin recognizes that she can calculate the market shares her sales director is asking for by first multiplying her sample's customer counts for each store by the average purchase size for each store and second, by dividing each of those three revenue totals by the sum of the three products. Max's market share, then, will be its own estimated average revenues for 88 sample customers divided by the sum of the products for the three stores.

She thinks that she can calculate an average sales volume per customer for Max's Farm Supply from internal sales records, but she is not confident that she can estimate the average per-customer purchase for Lowe's or Lawn & Garden, so she decides not to try to estimate market shares by sales volume for now. Estimating the average pesticide purchase per customer for Lowe's and Lawn & Garden, she concludes, represents a research project in its own right.

Robin summarizes her market share estimates with a pie chart to illustrate this division of the market by customer share rather than by revenue shares (Figure 13.3).

Linking Customer Behavior with Marketing Mix Decisions

In problem-solving research, an important association to examine is the relationship between buyers' decisions not to buy from you and your marketing mix decisions: pricing levels, product features, promotion activity, and distribution arrangements.

While devising her survey, Robin asks questions that allow the respondent to link his behavior or decisions to each store's pricing, product, advertising, or distribution choices. In making this asso-

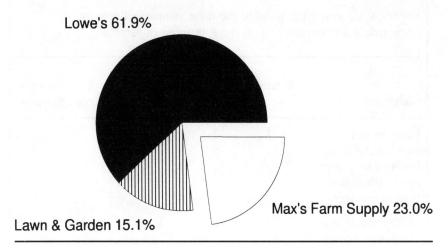

Lowe's 61.9%

Max's Farm Supply 23.0%

Lawn & Garden 15.1%

FIGURE 13.3 Market Shares

ciation, he explains why he did what he did in terms of factors the firm controls. For example, if customers are buying elsewhere, you must find out where they are buying, why they buy there instead of at your own place of business, and which criteria they used to compare the two businesses.

Robin has already identified where each respondent did most of his shopping in an earlier question. The questions in Figure 13.4 are linked to those choices. Responses to those questions are measured with attitude scales. Thus, the measures she has of their opinions are ordinal data only.

To summarize responses to these survey questions, Robin can use any of several techniques: medians or histograms by store or cross-tabulations (or "cross-tabs") of store with medians in the table cells (Table 13.3).

Because of the way Robin has decided to measure opinions in her scales, low median values (1s and 2s) indicate advantages for the store in question; 4s and 5s indicate disadvantages; 3s indicate neither advantage or disadvantage.

Have you ever shopped at Max's Farm Supply in (city, state)?

☐ No ☐ Yes

For the store you go to most of the time, please indicate the appropriate answer for each of the following questions:

Statement	Strongly agree	Agree	Neither agree or disagree	Disagree	Strongly disagree
I buy from (store) most of the time because its prices are much better than elsewhere.	1	2	3	4	5
I buy from (store) most of the time because its location is more convenient for me.	1	2	3	4	5
I buy from (store) most of the time because its service and product support is better than elsewhere.	1	2	3	4	5
I buy from (store) most of the time because its product quality and/or selection is better than elsewhere.	1	2	3	4	5
I buy from (store) in part due to the advertised specials and quality image.	1	2	3	4	5

FIGURE 13.4 Evaluating Store Attractions

TABLE 13.3   Marketing Mix Comparisons

	Median scale values				
Store	Pricing	Product	Convenience	Service	Advertising
Lowe's	1	2	3	4	2
Lawn & Garden	4	3	1	2	3
Max's Farm Supply	2	1	3	3	5

Robin analyzes this table. She interprets the results as indicating the following:

- Lowe's attracts its customers with advertising, low prices, and good product selections, but its customers also feel that this store's service and convenience are not outstanding.
- Lawn & Garden's customers are attracted by its convenient location and good service in spite of its relatively higher prices and more limited product choice. Advertising appears to be influential in attracting customers.
- Max's Farm Supply's customers are attracted by its good prices, excellent product selection, and excellent convenience. However, service quality is only average, and advertising is not a factor.

The survey question in Figure 13.4 asking whether survey respondents had ever shopped at Max's Farm Supply provides even more surprising results:

- Only 25 of the 237 respondents (10.5 percent) usually shopping at Lowe's had ever shopped at Max's Farm Supply.
- Only 5 of the 58 respondents (8.6 percent) usually shopping at Lawn & Garden had ever shopped at Max's Farm Supply.

This information implies to Robin that the crossover from the other two stores to Max's is very weak. Those customers have not considered Max's to be a good place to buy the products they get from their favored stores. The question is, why?

Robin wonders whether the benefits experienced by those buyers from their chosen stores are so much better or different than those experienced by Max's customers, whether the lack of advertising by Max's has contributed to a lack of awareness or knowledge about Max's offerings among these shoppers, or whether the image of Max's Farm Supply is too different from the lifestyles of those potential customers. As she analyzes the rest of her survey data, Robin intends to examine the ways in which the customers for her products are segmented among the three stores. In other words, she will try to understand the ways in which Max's customers differ from the customers of competitor stores. If they are clearly different, it may be that Max's will have trouble appealing to the types of customers attracted to Lowe's or Lawn & Garden.

Customer Satisfaction Measurements

Robin still needs to determine whether customers who have purchased a pesticide product at Max's are satisfied with the product and whether they have received good service and information about product use from Max's salespeople. Therefore, she adds the question shown in Figure 13.5 for respondents who have shopped at Max's.

The results to the question about customer satisfaction with product effectiveness illustrate that 23 percent of the sample have purchased a pesticide product from Max's Farm Supply within the past year. The responses from this 23 percent breaks down as follows:

- 65 percent: very satisfied
- 15 percent: satisfied
- 12 percent: neither satisfied nor dissatisfied
- 6 percent: moderately dissatisfied
- 2 percent: very dissatisfied

Have you purchased any pesticide or insect control products at Max's Farm Supply *within the past year?*

☐ Yes
☐ No

If you answered Yes above, we would like to ask how satisfied you were with the effectiveness of the product you bought. On a scale from 1 to 5, with 1 meaning very dissatisfied and 5 meaning very satisfied, how would you describe your satisfaction with the product?

     1   2   3   4   5

Now we would like to ask you about the quality of service from the salesperson you received with your purchase. On a scale from 1 to 5, with 1 meaning very poor service and 5 meaning very good service, how would you describe your satisfaction with the information and product support you received?

     1   2   3   4   5

FIGURE 13.5 Customer Satisfaction Questions

Robin feels that these results demonstrate strong consumer satisfaction with the effectiveness of the product line carried by Max's Farm Supply.

Responses to the question about satisfaction with salespersons' service with the sale, however, provide the following results:

- 25 percent: very satisfied
- 35 percent: satisfied
- 15 percent: neither satisfied nor dissatisfied
- 14 percent: dissatisfied
- 11 percent: very dissatisfied

She interprets these results less favorably than the previous satisfaction measures. Nearly half of these customers are less than completely satisfied with the service they received with their purchase.

Advertising Response

To assess the impact of competitor advertising, Robin includes a question to measure consumer awareness of Lowe's or Lawn & Garden advertising and subsequent response (Figure 13.6). The results were as follows:

- 95 respondents have noticed advertisements from Lowe's

Have you noticed advertisements about pesticide and insect control products locally?

　　☐ Yes
　　☐ No

If yes, who was the advertiser?

　　☐ Lowe's
　　☐ Lawn & Garden
　　☐ Other _____

Did you or a family member visit those stores and/or make a purchase of those products as a result of seeing those advertisements?

　　☐ Yes
　　☐ No

What was it about the advertisement that made you want to visit the store or purchase the product advertised?

_____

_____

_____

_____

FIGURE 13.6   Advertising Awareness (Unprompted)

- 37 respondents have noticed advertisements from Lawn & Garden
- 9 respondents reported having noticed advertisements from Max's Farm Supply

Of the 95 respondents citing ads from Lowe's, 27 indicated that they had responded with a visit or a purchase. Of the 37 respondents citing ads from Lawn & Garden, 15 indicated that they had responded with a visit or a purchase. All of the 9 respondents who reported seeing ads from Max's Farm Supply had visited or purchased from that store. (In fact, no advertisements had been run by Max's. These respondents were mistaken about having seen ads). A variety of other stores were also cited that did not sell these products as well.

The obviously erroneous responses regarding Max's advertising make Robin more cautious about accepting survey responses without question. As a result, she begins to look for internal consistency between the answers of each respondent. When she finds an error or a questionable response, she calls the person back and asks for a clarification.

The primary attraction cited for Lowe's ads is low prices. The primary attractions cited for Lawn & Garden are convenience and a good selection of light-duty equipment; flowers, trees, shrubs, and supplies for lawns and small gardens.

Customer Profiles

Robin feels she can gain even more insights into the ways the market is segmented by developing customer profiles for each store, so she includes a question on respondent age, sex, and income (Figure 13.7) in her questionnaire.

Customer Income Profiles   Robin reports the responses to these questions in a *frequency table* (Table 13.4). Only 6 percent of

We would also like to ask for information on your gender, age, and family income. We use this information only to classify our customers, which helps us understand their decisions better. We pledge to keep this information absolutely confidential; we will not release this information outside the company and will not link your name with your answers in our files.

(Please check appropriate categories)

Sex:
☐ Male
☐ Female

Earned family income:
☐ Below $10,000 a year
☐ $10,000 to $19,999 a year
☐ $20,000 to $29,999 a year
☐ $30,000 to $39,999 a year
☐ $40,000 or more a year

Age of respondent:
☐ Less than 20 years of age
☐ 20 to 29 years of age
☐ 30 to 39 years of age
☐ 40 to 49 years of age
☐ 50 to 59 years of age
☐ 60 years of age or more

User status:
☐ Farmer
☐ Landscaping
☐ Plant nursery
☐ Home use only
☐ Other _____

FIGURE 13.7   Client Characteristics

respondents reported family incomes of less than $20,000 per year, and about equal shares reported incomes in the $20,000-to-$29,999, $30,000-to-$39,999, and $40,000-plus ranges.

Robin then wants to know the income and sex of the major customers of each store. She first uses her survey data to perform a cross-tabulation between the data from her income question and the data from her market share question (Table 13.5).

Why are marketing researchers interested in income? Because small businesspeople must find out where the money is to buy their products. Families with higher incomes spend more, and they are in many cases more likely to buy high-quality products and services that carry higher prices.

TABLE 13.4 Income Distribution of the Market

Income category	Number of responses	Percent distribution
Less than $20,000 a year	20	6
$20,000 to $29,999 a year	105	31
$30,000 to $39,999 a year	105	31
$40,000 or more a year	108	32
Total	338	100

Note: Forty-five respondents were units of local government and small retail outlets. These responses were removed.

TABLE 13.5 Cross-Tab of Income on Store Patronized

Income category	Lowe's		Lawn & Garden		Max's Farm Supply		Column totals	
	No.	%	No.	%	No.	%	No.	%
Less than $20,000	5	2	7	14	8	11	20	6
$20,000 to $29,999	29	14	27	52	49	68	105	31
$30,000 to $39,999	88	41	9	17	8	11	105	31
$40,000 or more	92	43	9	17	7	10	108	32
Row Total	214	100	52	100	72	100	338	100

Note: The columns of this table represent the income distributions of the customers of each store. Responses from government and retailers removed from table.

In Table 13.5, the survey data on income and patronage reveals the relationship between this customer characteristic and customers' behavior (patronizing one store more than others). In the example, Lowe's is attracting 84 percent of its customers from families having incomes equal to or more than $30,000 a year. Lawn & Garden gets 66 percent of its customers from families receiving incomes of less than $30,000. Finally, 79 percent of Max's Farm Supply's customers' families earn less than $30,000 a year in income.

From these results, Robin recognizes how Lowe's had positioned itself in the higher-income segment of the market by choosing a strategic location, advertising, and merchandising skills. Max's is attracting mostly lower-income families.

Customer Gender Profile   The results of Robin's tabulations on gender revealed that males represent 75 percent of these respondents. But when she cross-tabulates gender data with data on the store most patronized by respondents, she gets the results displayed in Table 13.6.

These results establish for Robin that the customers of Max's Farm Supply, like those of Lowe's, are largely male. Lawn & Garden, however, primarily caters to women customers. This information, she knows, will be important for understanding the important differences between the marketing programs of the three competitors.

TABLE 13.6   Cross-Tab of Sex on Store Choice

Sex	Lowe's Actual	%	Lawn & Garden Actual	%	Max's Farm Supply Actual	%	Column total Actual	%
Males	180	84	15	29	59	82	254	75
Females	34	16	37	71	13	18	84	25
Totals	214	100	52	100	72	100	338	100

Note: Government and retail responses have been omitted.

Product User Profile   Robin has also requested information on respondent occupation or buyer status in her questionnaire. With her computer, Robin prepares a cross-tab of the survey responses for this question. The results are displayed in Table 13.7.

From this data, she realizes that Max's share of purchases from farmers was only 40 percent. She recalls the comment from one of Max's salespeople that farmers had made up 60 percent of the purchasers last year. Now Robin realizes that she has made a mistake in constructing her questionnaire by not asking if each respondent had purchased Max's brand of pesticides last year but had since changed to another brand and if so, why? But it was too late to get that information now that the survey was over—or was it?

Robin seeks to get that information in another way. She looks up each of the farmers in her sample who was purchasing from either Lowe's or Lawn & Garden, calls each one on the telephone, and asks her question. Overwhelmingly, the answers are that they have heard or seen warnings about the active ingredients of Max's

TABLE 13.7   Store Customer Profile

Categories	Lowe's No.	Lowe's %	Lawn & Garden No.	Lawn & Garden %	Max's Farm Supply No.	Max's Farm Supply %	Row totals No.	Row totals %
Farmers	25	11	2	4	40	45	67	17
Nurseries	3	1	2	4	20	23	25	7
Landscaping	10	4	2	4	8	9	20	5
Home use only	176	74	46	78	4	5	226	59
Others	23[1]	10[1]	6	10	16[2]	18[2]	45	12
Totals	237	100	58	100	88	100	383	100

[1]*Note:* These were units of local government; Lowe's had negotiated a favorable price for a number of municipalities and government agencies.

[2]*Note:* These customers were primarily small retailers who purchased these products in small quantities for their stores in surrounding small towns and crossroad stores in rural areas.

brand and have switched their purchases to competing stores. In fact, they have done business with Max's for years, and if a safer product were available, they would buy it from Max's because of the quantity discounts and delivery service.

CONCLUSIONS OF THE STUDY

Robin's conclusions for her study of Max's decline in pesticide sales are as follows:

- *From her comparisons of prices of comparable products,* she concludes that prices on Max's product line are almost identical among all the major competitors for small quantities. However, Max's is the only retailer that offers quantity discounts. Max's Farm Supply is a favorite of large-scale users such as farmers and nurseries because of this pricing and because Max's delivers.
- *From her survey,* she finds that buyers of Max's products are satisfied with the effectiveness of their purchases in controlling pests in gardens and fields and around the house.
- *From her visits to competitor stores,* she finds that new brands on their shelves are doing very well and are gaining ground on the brand carried by Max's Farm Supply.
- *Her customer survey* produces market share measures showing that brands sold by competitors are also doing quite well, in part due to advertising and special promotions on those brands by Lowe's and Lawn & Garden.
- *From her survey,* she finds that nonfarm customers are still using the products for gardens and have no complaints, but farm customers are beginning to discontinue their use of this product line because of concerns about possible damage to livestock and wild animals.
- *Her letter to the Environmental Protection Agency* generates the response that EPA studies of this product are causing a review of current regulations on its use in agriculture.

- *Conversations with her university extension office* reveal that the extension service has been urging area farmers to discontinue their use of these products and switch to less toxic brands. Although the EPA has not yet banned use of these products in agriculture, it is expected to. Farm organizations have been warning farmers to switch to several other brands.
- *From her customer survey,* she finds that many buyers have noticed advertising and promotions from the other stores. Many have tried competitor products as a result of those advertisements.
- *From her survey of competitors' customers,* she discovers that very high proportions of those customers have never shopped at Max's and therefore are unlikely to be able to effectively compare Max's with their current store.
- *From her study of ad clippings,* she notes that the advertising by Lowe's and Lawn & Garden demonstrated awareness of a strongly segmented market in the local area. This segmentation had left Max's with a rural farm and institutional market. Advertisements from both competitors, however, feature many other convenient and labor-saving lawn care and gardening products. Neither of the other competitors features farming equipment or heavy-duty supplies.
- *From her telephone calls to the manufacturers of the products being sold by Max's and the other competitors,* she found that the new products being introduced by competitors are less toxic than Max's current products and have had few complaints filed with the Environmental Protection Agency. Manufacturers of those products still carried by Max's are adamant that nothing is wrong with their product and that EPA reviews are "a tempest in a teapot."
- *From her analysis of internal sales records,* she discovers that sales force performance has dipped. Conversations with those salespeople result in a suspicion that two of the four salespeople are confused by the restrictions on product use and product direc-

tions and have not been adequately trained to provide good advice and information to customers.

- *From survey data inquiring about product service in the pesticide products,* poor service and inadequate product knowledge by Max's salespeople in this product line have resulted in some of those customers beginning to shop at competitor stores.

RECOMMENDATIONS

When Robin makes her report to you (remember, you are the president of Max's Farm Supply) and your sales director, she includes the following recommendations:

- Cut back shelf space and inventory in the old product line and decrease sales quotas on this product to meet nonfarm demand only.
- Plan new product introductions that will comply with EPA guidelines and meet the new needs in the farm market. Sell only products that have the endorsement of the university agricultural extension service. (She lists several brands suggested by the extension service for your consideration.)
- Emphasize the farm market and other large-volume customers in new product introductions and promotions. The farm market is your store's traditional and strongest market. However, investigate the potential of contracts with area governments as well. Your delivery capability may give you an advantage over Lowe's in the rural areas.
- Make no price changes in the old product line or changes in product features.
- Consider product advertising directed toward the rural population to enhance public awareness of the new product lines. A direct mail promotion to farmers letting them know you have the new products will let them know you are staying up with the latest EPA guidelines.

- Consider advertising tests in the local paper to increase public awareness of the store and its unique offerings in the area. In those advertisements, feature products of interest to those market segments.
- Provide training for sales staff to improve their technical knowledge of both the old and any new product lines.

REPORTING ON RESEARCH RESULTS

If the decision maker and the research analyst are one and the same, a written report may not be important except as a useful summary for later reference when revising the marketing plan. However, if the analyst is a consultant or perhaps an employee of the decision maker, then reporting is important.

Decision makers generally prefer short reports that note the important conclusions and perhaps summarize the major reasons for those conclusions. Provide a brief executive summary for the decision makers. A more complete report may also be required with the following format:

1. Title page
2. Table of contents
3. Executive summary
4. Introduction
5. Conclusions and recommendations
6. Chapters on analysis and data

    A. Methodology

    B. Analysis

    C. Assumptions and limitations of study

7. Appendixes

Many decision makers will also desire an oral report. Here are several suggestions that should help to make an oral presentation go well:

- Limit any presentation to 20 to 30 minutes
- Use visual displays, overhead projections, slides, and even flip charts to limit lengthy text or verbal explanations; put text into very brief "bullets"
- Stand up as you make the presentation
- Allow for questions and answers from the decision makers after your presentation
- Present your recommendations as alternatives for the decision makers—not as "the decisions you should make." Explain the pros and cons of each alternative course of action.

MAKING MARKETING RESEARCH A HABIT

14

At the dawn of the twenty-first century, economic insecurities seem to be intensifying. Student counselors are telling their charges to prepare for four to five major career changes during their working lives. We hear that each of us must constantly upgrade our skills or retrain for new jobs. Around us, huge corporations are crashing, while hundreds of thousands of workers are dispossessed each year from their jobs. In the computer markets, the pace of technological advancement makes obsolete the products of only six months past. The world is a very different place than it was 20 or even 10 years ago.

THE IMPACT OF ACCELERATING CHANGES

The pace of change has another important impact on the small businessperson: Our understanding of our markets as well as our niche in them is as mortal as we are. Thus, the accuracy of the information or knowledge we base our plans on has only a limited life. And year by year as we prepare to enter the twenty-first century, the lifespan of that knowledge is getting shorter and shorter.

It is no accident, for example, that during the second half of the twentieth century, the concept of "strategic," or long-term plans became popular in corporate America. Business, beset by accelerating change, began to look further down the road in an attempt to stay on the road, much the same way a driver must when his vehicle accelerates its speed. The faster we go, the further ahead we must peer to make sure we can turn or brake in time in the event the road turns or someone else merges onto the road.

MAKE TIME FOR LIFELONG LEARNING

Driving the roads of the next century will doubtlessly require new driving skills. We already see some of them in the field of marketing research: understanding of statistical analysis, marketing concepts such as market segmentation and database marketing, computer operating skills, software programming skills, and surfing the Internet. But even more than technical skills, there is a need for thinking people—people who can solve problems.

As businesspeople, each of us must find ways of keeping up with the information in our fields and even starting new careers. Many of the skills discussed in this book are not commonly included even in college business programs. And within ten years, perhaps a good number of the skills discussed here will be out of use and replaced by other, more efficient methods.

The answer is probably to stay active in some kind of continuing education program. Seek out those courses that will give you the skills to understand your customers, your markets, and your business.

Avoid the trap of pursuing too narrow an educational target. Read the writings of the futurists—Alvin Toffler's *The Third Wave* (New York: Bantam Books, 1981) as well as *Powershift* (New York:

Bantam Books, 1990) and Daniel Burrus's *Technotrends* (New York: Harper Business, 1993)—and try to peer ahead with them to anticipate the world of the future. Keep up with the economic and political trends of the day and try to understand the forces that move them. Toffler's view that everything that happens is part of a larger mosaic is a useful perspective to keep in mind. Remember that your business, your market, your niche, and your profits are transitory unless you learn to change with the times.

If you can find a marketing research course or two, take them. Look especially into the art of conducting surveys. Consider courses in psychology and sociology as preparation for focus group and individual interviewing and, of course, take any marketing courses you can find. Learning about your markets and your customers must become part of your continuing education.

NOTHING HAPPENS UNTIL YOU ACT

This continuing educational effort has to be directed at creating a successful business. It is true that this educational program is providing "research skills," but the notion must be discarded that research has nothing to do with the real world. In a world characterized by risk, the best way for a small businessperson to manage that risk is by seeking knowledge. In a world characterized by increasing risk, that knowledge will have to be gained through changing the paradigms of learning. Technology is driving much of the changes, but it is also providing the means to leverage time and lower costs in the gathering and sorting of information so that unwanted information does not come to us.

Education can get you ready to learn about your market, but it won't teach you what you need to know about the market. So get the tools you need. Use them to find your market and to penetrate it. All the research in the world, however, won't make a dollar for you if you don't use what you learn to make better decisions and take action.

Nothing happens until you take action!

NOTES

CHAPTER 1

1. Amar Bhide, "How Entrepreneurs Craft Strategies That Work," in *Harvard Business Review* 72 (March-April 1994): 152.
2. Ibid.
3. J. B. McKitterick, "What Is the Marketing Management Concept?" in *The Frontiers of Marketing Thought and Science,* ed. Frank M. Bass (Chicago: American Marketing Association, 1957), 79.
4. Dik Warren Twedt, *1978 Survey of Marketing Research* (Chicago: American Marketing Association, 1978), 41.
5. Adapted from E. Jerome McCarthy, *Basic Marketing: A Managerial Approach,* 7th ed. (Homewood, Ill: Richard D. Irwin, 1981), 52.

CHAPTER 3

1. Gilbert A. Churchill, *Marketing Research: Methodological Foundations* (Chicago: The Dryden Press, 1983), 59–65.

CHAPTER 5

1. Lois Horowitz, "Researching from Magazines and Reference Books," in *Handbook of Magazine Article Writing,* ed. Jean M. Fredette (Cincinnati: Writer's Digest Books, 1988), 27–33.

CHAPTER 6

1. "Pathfinders being sought to redefine on-line world" by Kius Jensen, Cox News Service, in "The News and Observer," Business Section, November 29, 1994, p. 3D.
2. *Home Office Computing,* December 1994, p. 14.

CHAPTER 8

1. Jeffrey L. Pope, *Practical Marketing Research* (New York: AMA COM, 1981), 21–23.
2. MPM Associates, *The Marketing Plan: How to Prepare It ... What Should Be in It?* (Towson, MD: MPM Associates, 1978).
3. Rob Jackson and Paul Wang, *Strategic Database Marketing.* (Lincolnwood, IL: NTC Business Books, 1994), 27.

CHAPTER 9

1. Arthur M. Hughes, *Strategic Database Marketing* (Chicago: Probus Publishing Company, 1994), 64.
2. Don Debelak, *Marketing Magic,* (Holbrook, MA: Bob Adams, Inc., 1994), 65–66.
3. Ibid., 66.
4. Ibid.

CHAPTER 10

1. Hughes, *Strategic Database Marketing,* 15.
2. Jackson and Wang, *Strategic Database Marketing,* 89–95.
3. Ibid.
4. Hughes, *Strategic Database Marketing,* 3.
5. Ibid., 87–104.

6. Ibid., 107–132.
7. Jackson and Wang, *Strategic Database Marketing*, 41–44.

CHAPTER 11

1. Pope, *Practical Marketing Research*, 32.
2. Ibid., 36–40.

CHAPTER 12

1. Churchill, *Marketing Research*, 190–95.
2. Pope, *Practical Marketing Research*, 28–29.
3. Ibid., 29.
4. Jane Farley Templeton, *Focus Groups: A Guide for Marketing or Advertising Professionals* (Chicago: Probus Publishing, 1987), 144–163.
5. Ibid., 144.
6. Ibid., 30.

CHAPTER 13

1. Churchill, *Marketing Research*, 22.

INDEX